HOW HARD ARE YOU KNOCKING?

LANDING A JOB IN A REBOUNDING ECONOMY

Third Edition

by
Timothy J. Augustine
With Lisa Mangigian

ISBN:1-4637-3895-1

ISBN-13:978-1-4637-3895-2

Library of Congress Control Number: 2011912687

Createspace, North Charleston SC

ACKNOWLEDGEMENTS

Special thanks to our friends and family for their continued love and support. In addition, there are a number of people who provided advice, shared best practices and supplied valuable research to help bring this book to print. Thanks to Hal Becker, Weston Bruner, Adam Carroll, Mark Chiacchiari, Elizabeth Freedman, Joel Graves, Candice Hancock, Thomas Hauck, Dipak Jain, John Jimenez, Shyam Kambeyanda, Nick Mangigian, Mary Olson-Menzel, Laura Turner, and Corinna Weller. We would also like to thank the University of Michigan and acknowledge our focus group that helped transform the research into reality. They include: Emily Gwinn, Melissa Morof, Yu Zhou, Mark Wilhelm, Jessica Soley, Nicholas Taylor, Yuning Zhang, Nickolas Laws, Kelli Huntsman, Caitlin Gdowski, Melissa Morof, Liliya Arutyunyan, Jeany Zhang, and Michelle Kang.

TABLE OF CONTENTS

FORWARD i

CHAPTER 1: ARE YOU READY FOR A JOB SEARCH? 1

Dream Jobs and Dream Cars 2

Key Questions 4

CHAPTER 2: WHY SHOULD I HIRE YOU? 7

CHAPTER 3: WHERE DO YOU WANT TO WORK? 17

Determine Key Company Criteria 24

Job Search Strategy: Twenty Key Questions and Your Best Answers 28

Real-Life Examples: Ben vs. Susan 32

CHAPTER 4: WHAT INFORMATION DO YOU NEED? 37

Career Centers (Community or University) 37

Internet 40

Professional Association/Organization Websites 42

Professional Organizations 43

Professional Recruiting Firms 44

Staffing and Temporary Firms 48

Print Media 52

CHAPTER 5: WHO DO YOU KNOW? WHO KNOWS YOU? 55

College and University Networking Events 59

Business Cards 61

Prepare Your Thirty-Second Commercial 62

Informational Interviews 63

Script for Cold Calling for an Informational Interview 64

Dress for Success 69

Your Professional Attitude 69

Develop Your Professional Identity 71

Build Your Professional Brand 73

Who Knows You Online? 74

CHAPTER 6: WHERE ARE YOU IN YOUR JOB SEARCH? 77

CHAPTER 7: SELLING YOURSELF 81

Appearance Matters 82

Content Matters 84

Key Sections of the Resume 85

Work and Related Experience Examples 97

Leadership Experience 99

Connect the Dots with Your Cover Letter 104

CHAPTER 8: HOW DO YOU LOOK? 129

Basic Rules...129

For Women 131

For Men...136

For Men and Women..139

CHAPTER 9: THE INTERVIEW 141

Tell Me About Yourself 142

The Four Types of Interviews...............................143

Interview Topics 162

Sample Interview Questions 167

Preparation/Practice for the Interview.......................177

The Interview 180

Follow-Up After the Interviews 187

CHAPTER 10: CLOSING THE DEAL........................... 191

Next Steps and Expectations................................191

Rejection 192

Negotiation and Acceptance 194

Accepting an Offer 201

CHAPTER 11: DID YOU CHOOSE THE RIGHT JOB? 209

The First 90 Days...210

Master the Company..211

Master Your Position 212

Master the Company Product and/or Services.............................213

Master the Company Politics 215

Master Your Own Professional Effectiveness 216

Personal Satisfaction 219

Professional Development..219

Financial Reward..220

CHAPTER 12: MANAGING YOUR CAREER 223

Stay Connected with Your Network...223

Stay Connected to Your Industry and Profession 224

Continue to Build Your Personal Effectiveness Skills 225

Update Your Master Resume at Least Once a Year 225

A Tale of Two Job Seekers: Susan vs. Mike 225

ADDITIONAL ENDORSEMENTS

"This latest edition of How Hard Are You Knocking? is a must-have for new and experienced job-seekers alike. The book takes a comprehensive approach to securing a job in today's challenging and competitive economy. It will prove to a be a valuable resource to anybody that reads it and follows its guidance."

– Mark Chiacchiari - Grand President,International
Fraternity of Delta Sigma Pi

"The How Hard Are You Knocking series will be the next job search bible. Augustine empowers the job seeker with critical information needed in today's competitive job market."

– Mary Olson-Menzel - Partner, Ascend Executive Search

"How Hard Are You Knocking is a must-read for job-seeking college students. This helpful manual offers plenty of practical tips, useful advice, and details so that you'll know exactly what you have to do to land an opportunity."

– Elizabeth Freedman - Author, *Work 101: Learning the Ropes of the*
Workplace without Hanging Yourself

"Tim is a high energy, creative, and impactful career development expert! He delivers a straight, no-nonsense message to recent graduates and seasoned professionals with the right mix of humor and levity.

University of Michigan students and alumni love his approach and practical application of knowledge."

– Laura Turner - Senior Career Manager, Alumni Association
of the University of Michigan

"In today's global economy, job seekers need a competitive edge to give them confidence, knowledge and the ability to compete. *Knocking* is the best resource available for new job seekers who want to differentiate themselves in this evolving economy. You will use this book for the rest of your career."

– Shyam Kambeyanda - General Manager, Eaton India

"As a senior in college, I had no idea what to expect going into the job market. I would never have gotten the job I have- or perhaps any job- without the help of this book. It is a perfect summary of everything you need to know to find a job. How Hard Are You Knocking doesn't just tell you what you need to do, but why you need to do it and more importantly, what the interviewer will be thinking before, during, and after the interview. Tim and Lisa truly understand the emotional and mental toll of the interviewing process, and provide their readers not only with tips and tricks, but a comprehensive plan for how to approach any interview and the job search in general. Regardless of whether you are looking to work in the non-profit, for-profit, or any other field, this advice is invaluable"

– Weston Bruner - University of Michigan Graduate 2009
Development Research Analyst

"The perfect book for job seekers in today's rebounding economy. A fantastic resource for anyone looking for a new job. Detailed, concise and full of great tools that will guide the job seekers through the entire process of landing their dream job."

— Adam Carroll - Best Selling Author, *The Money Game*

FORWARD

In today's challenging job market, many job seekers are facing stiff competition, fewer job postings and job opportunities, and a skittish business environment filled with uncertainty and fear. Job seekers today are dealing with an economic recession which transcends all demographics, industries, and experience levels causing anxiety, job search fatigue and frustration. With these challenges, the job market has experienced a significant increase in competition requiring job seekers to understand their skills and abilities to position themselves in the right situation and differentiate themselves in the competitive market.

Looking for a job can be stressful, and today's market isn't helping. The job market has been hit the hardest during this global recession and severe economic downturn in the last few years. Fortunately, there are signs of growth and economic recovery. *How Hard Are You Knocking? Landing a Job in a Rebounding Economy* is a process oriented guide that will walk you, the job seeker, through the entire job-search process from building your job search strategy, identifying your target companies, negotiating a starting salary and finally succeeding in your new job.

For the last few years, we have been researching the job market, geographic areas, and multiple industries that have been significantly impacted by the economic downturn. We have studied growth markets and industries projected to expand in the next five to ten years. We have conducted extensive research with hiring executives in order to understand their hiring criteria, candidate expectations, and growth plans for the future. We have led focus groups consisting of college students, entry-level candidates, and experienced job seekers and have conducted seminars and workshops for job seekers around the country. Finally, as business owners, we have interviewed thousands and hired hundreds of candidates at all levels in various geographic regions throughout the US, Europe and Asia. Through this extensive research and market intelligence, we have developed a thorough yet-concise guide that will help you land a job.

Today's job seekers need to identify what they want to do, where they want to work, and understand how their unique skills satisfy those organizations looking to fill new openings. Companies are looking for value and want to see a quick return on their investment when they make hiring decisions. Therefore, it's required by the job seeker, not the employer, to identify the value they bring during the interview.

As the economy begins to climb out of the recession, the job market will begin to rebound. Job seekers who are prepared and have a plan in place will be in the best position to land their dream job.

Using this book as a guide, you will be able to begin building your job search strategy. You should begin your plan by targeting specific industries and companies. Once identified, you can conduct your research to uncover internship and job opportunities by leveraging your network, various career resources and utilizing social media. You will also find techniques on landing the first impression, creating a targeted result oriented resume, and developing your interview skills. We have included a comprehensive list of the most commonly asked situational interview questions along with the best answers we feel will differentiate you during the interview process.

With this book, you will have the confidence and ability to land the job you desire. We will guide you along the way and be your secret weapon throughout the process.

WHAT'S IN THE BOOK?

We begin the process by helping you develop an overall job search strategy. What are the skills you bring to a company? What are the valued attributes you pride yourself in offering a company? There are seven key steps that will serve as your roadmap to land your dream job:

STEP I: IDENTIFY WHAT YOU WANT TO DO.

This step is dedicated to helping you identify your specific interests, skills, and abilities and matching them to target industries and companies. As you're building your strategy, you need to identify what makes you unique and what you bring to the company. Once you have identified what makes you unique, you need to identify the industries you really want to be a part of and have a passion for. Maybe it's an industry that offers local presence and opportunity or an urgent industry that is growing during this economic cycle. We're going to provide you with tools that you can use to identify those industries as well as those target companies.

STEP 2: RESEARCH WHERE YOU WANT TO WORK.

The next step is doing your homework by conducting research to learn and understand the most important aspects of an organization. It's critically important that <u>before</u> you start developing your résumé and start preparing for the interview, you understand what the company is all about. Our strategy is to help you identify 10 - 15 organizations you want to work for. It is then your responsibility to do as much homework on those organizations as possible. Your research should include identifying locations, the types of products and services the company provides, an understanding of the market it serves and the firm's organizational structure. We'll provide different tools, websites, and techniques you can use to uncover the whole corporate picture.

STEP 3: LEARN HOW TO DISCOVER AND UNCOVER JOB OPPORTUNITIES.

The next step is learning how to uncover job opportunities. In this section, we will help you leverage career development tools such as internet job boards, company research, informational interviews, industry associations, and strategies to navigate a career fair or tradeshow.

The most powerful resource you have as a job seeker is your personal and professional network. We will help you develop strategies to build your network, and learn best practices to leverage it during your job search.

STEP 4: UNDERSTAND HOW TO MAKE A POSITIVE FIRST IMPRESSION.

The next step is making a good first impression. The first impression can be influenced by the candidate's professional attire, attention to detail, and preparation for the interview. In this section, we will explore gender specific attire most suitable for the interview as well as the details that will differentiate you as a candidate. We will also provide specific rules for building your résumé and preparing for the interview process. Your résumé should sell you and your abilities, match the criteria on the position description and be customized to the industry as well as your target company. We are focused on this type of process because it's critically important for you to differentiate yourself as a job seeker.

In today's job market, you will face various competitors. Not only are you facing peers, but you are also facing experienced individuals who have been laid-off in this downturn and who are willing to take less money and open to multiple positions, if needed, to get back in the job market. You are also facing global competition. The world is truly flat, thus you are competing with not only domestic individuals but the international marketplace as well. In today's job market, companies are very skittish about making significant hires or adding too many people. When they do post a position, they are very selective in who they hire. Therefore, you need to find every way to differentiate yourself and position yourself as the best candidate for the job.

This book will explore the different types of interviews you're going to face – a phone interview, a meal interview, a group interview, and a face-to-face interview. We will explore the types of situational questions that will be asked and optimal answers hiring executives are looking for.

STEP 5: DEVELOP A STRATEGY TO EVALUATE OPPORTUNITIES.

Once you have conducted the first few interviews and moved into the final round, you will need to develop a strategy to review the best opportunities. We will teach you what you need to ask during your second and third interviews and specific information you should uncover which will help you evaluate opportunities such as health care premiums, 401k matches, tuition reimbursement, the type of compensation and benefits the company provides. We will also provide you with specific questions to ask during these interviews such as "How are performance reviews conducted?" or "How are promotions evaluated?" These types of questions should be asked in the second and third interviews to paint the entire picture while you're deciding on an opportunity. Finally, we will explore proven techniques to negotiate your salary, which can form a foundation for future wage increases and promotions.

STEP 6: SUCCEED ONCE YOU LAND THE JOB.

Once you land the job, *How Hard Are You Knocking* will help you build an effective orientation, transition strategy and career development plan. We will focus on the first 90 days of employment and provide specific strategies to understand the five most important components of a firm to help you successfully transition into the firm and begin making your impact. These components include company history, products, processes, politics and your personal goals. Company knowledge explores the company's history and outlines the company's strategy and long-term direction. Product and services knowledge explores what the company produces or provides to their clients. Process knowledge highlights how things are done and how the company operates. Political knowledge provides a framework for the political environment and strategies to navigate the politics of the company. The final area of focus is personal effectiveness, which focuses on your career growth and long-term career plan.

STEP 7: LEARN HOW TO CONTINUE KNOCKING THROUGHOUT YOUR CAREER.

In the final section, we will provide strategies to help grow your career and position yourself for long-term success. There are three specific areas of your life that should be fulfilled. The first is personal satisfaction, which needs to be present in a balanced life. Your job and life should include enjoyment, fun, a sense of belonging, happiness, love, and celebration. The second area is professional growth, which includes accomplishment, learning, growing, experiencing new things, stretching, and setting goals. The final area that should be present in a balanced life is financial reward, which includes salary, wage, benefits and total compensation. If you are happy and growing in your career, money will follow. We hope this section enables you to continue to grow and prosper in your new job and future career.

In summary, *How Hard Are You Knocking* is designed to walk job seekers through the entire job search process, from building an initial strategy to doing research and then identifying the industry and target companies. Job seekers will also learn strategies to develop a powerful résumé, techniques to leverage their network, tools to prepare for all types of interviews, and techniques to make a positive first impression. Finally, we will cover appropriate attire to land the first impression, strategies to negotiate a starting salary and tips for building your career after you land your job.

We hope you enjoy *How Hard Are You Knocking*. We hope it is as meaningful to you as it has been to research and develop, and we look forward to keeping in touch throughout your career. Good luck.

CHAPTER 1

ARE YOU READY FOR A JOB SEARCH?

Throughout our research, we found one common denominator among successful job seekers. That common denominator is preparation. Whether you are evaluating your target positions, researching growth industries, connecting with your personal or professional network or simply putting the final touches on your resume, the key to a successful job hunt is preparation. As you prepare for your unique job search, the first critical step is to understand yourself and evaluate your strengths, weaknesses, passions, interests, and unique skills that you bring to a position and company. A job hunt first begins with understanding yourself. After all, only you know what you want and who you are. Not until you have assessed your strengths, preferences, and motivations can you take the next step and explore all of your options and opportunities. If this sounds like too much pressure, rest assured, we can help you through every step and keep you accountable in making progress. We believe that the tools, techniques, and strategies outlined in this book will help you solidify your goals, identify your unique value proposition and help you land your dream job.

We broke down the entire job search process into step-by-step chapters that provides you with the necessary information such as the

1

expectations of a hiring manager, best practices from success stories and insider's tips for each step along the way. There are also assignments and chapter checklists to keep you on track. We understand the difficulty of the job search process and we don't want to sugarcoat this challenge. At times, you will feel frustrated and even encounter some setbacks. The job search process can be stressful. Use this guide to help you navigate the process and provide you with the confidence needed to compete in a challenging market.

Job hunting is an active sport; it's not for the faint of heart! We want you to be fully informed before you begin. You will need to do some preparation work prior to starting your search such as an internal assessment. An internal assessment is a tool that forces you to consider, analyze and answer specific questions about your unique skills, abilities and interests. We have found that this assessment is one of the most important first steps you can make to build a winning strategy.

How are you approaching your job search?

DREAM JOBS AND DREAM CARS

We have found that some job hunters put less effort into finding a job than they spend seeking out their dream car. Some job hunters simply open the classified section of the local paper or view listings through an online job board and see what catches their eye. There is no forethought put into the process. Now, can you imagine this same process with car buying? Would you just open up the classifieds and see what cars are available without having any previously determined criteria? Or would you consider your needs for safety and reliability as well as price? Would you review the warranty before purchasing? Would you choose the vehicle based on the photo or the features? Wouldn't it be hard to make a good decision? Wouldn't you rather first think about what you need before looking at your options?

Purchasing a car is a big investment and should be handled with due diligence. We think job hunters also need to develop thoughtful criteria. They need to know their preferences before looking at the options. Otherwise, they can get distracted and fall into a job that is not a good fit for their skills, interests and values. When job hunters enter the job market with full knowledge of their preferences and needs, they are more likely to find positions that are professionally satisfying and have the ability to differentiate themselves from their competition.

Instead of a random approach to job-hunting, we suggest that you carefully consider ten key career questions answered in the chapters of this book:

1. Why should you be hired?
2. Where do you want to work?
3. What information do you need?
4. Who do you know?
5. Who knows you?
6. Can you sell yourself?
7. Do you look the part?
8. Can you close the deal?
9. Did you choose the right job?

10. How will you manage your career?

In this book, we will answer these questions and prepare you to conduct a successful job search.

First, let's look at whether you are really ready for a job search.

KEY QUESTIONS

Ask yourself the **why, where, what** and **when** questions related to your job search.

Figure out **why** you are contemplating a job change right now. Are you really ready? Also ask yourself the **where** question. Do you have any geographical preferences? Are you willing to move? Will you conduct a national or international job search? Or are you bound to home because of responsibilities and family preferences? As for **what** job, the first step is to identify and research an industry, the companies and then the specific positions. You also need to know **when** you'll be available for work now, or after graduation.

What are your options?

Do you want to work full-time or part-time? Do you want to start a company, work at a start-up company, or work for an established organization? Would you consider a temporary job? Would volunteering be a good place to start to gain experience and make contacts? Do you want to make a job change, career transition or do you need help determining what you want to do in your career?

4

These may seem like a lot of questions, but if you are able to answer most of these questions, you will now have a clear focus to develop your job search strategy.

Chapter Checklist

✓ I understand that I need to approach my job search very diligently focused on my goals and interests.

✓ I am willing to approach my job search in an organized and strategic manner.

✓ I have begun to answer the preparation questions and am ready to build my job search strategy.

✓ I know what I need in a job to be personally and professionally satisfied.

A note about chapter checklists: These checklists are to keep you on track. Before reading ahead, take time to consider and attend to these checkpoints!

CHAPTER 2

WHY SHOULD I HIRE YOU?

In this chapter, you will be pushed and prodded to ask a brutally honest question about yourself: **Why are you a better candidate than your best friend?** To answer this question you need to do the hard work of assessing and understanding your skills, strengths, personality, and work styles. You need to get real with yourself. If you hate biology, get off the track to a medical career. If you want to work with people, figure what types of people and how you want to work with them. Do you want to provide a service, sell a product, or affect their behavior? After gathering data on yourself, you can start to articulate your competitive advantage. Only then can you start looking for a job.

The first step of the job search is to **look inside and assess your strengths**. Only you can figure out what qualities, skills and assets differentiate you from the competition. The following ten areas can be used as a guide for this assessment. Use it to document your goals, identify your career target, and develop steps to help you reach those goals. This activity serves two purposes.

First, it forces you to think more carefully about your goals as you convert your desires into words.

Second, it provides a constant reminder and reference as you move forward in your job search process.

Look back at this list in later years and amend it as your career and life goals change.

This exercise is designed to uncover your own internal drivers. Internal drivers are those passions, skills, and attributes that pique one's interest and maintain the curiosity to continue to learn more. By identifying your internal drivers, you will be able to assess different positions and companies and establish your career direction. Ask yourself these questions and write down your answers. Feel free to list several answers to each question in bullet-point form. The idea is to get the thoughts down on paper and out of your mind. Honesty is important here. If, for example, you want to be close to your family most of the time, don't write down that you want a job that includes 75 percent travel.

Insider's Tip: Internal drivers are the motivating values or principles that direct your life and thus will impact your career choices. A driver could be time with family or it could be earning enough money to live very comfortably. These are the underlying principles that may even guide your life subconsciously. Now is the time to dig deep to discover them so they can help you on your career path.

This process will also help you identify the type of firm you would like to work for, the type of culture that you would thrive in, and the unique skills you can bring to a new position. Based on our experience, the number one reason that a new employee leaves a firm within six months is cultural misalignment. If you follow this exercise, you should be able to identify the types of companies where you can thrive.

In one case, our firm had hired a sales manager with a great deal of experience. Prior to joining our small firm, he worked with three large multi-national companies, where he was very successful. After a series of interviews, we selected him as our top candidate and offered him the job. Within the first month, we began to see a problem. Our culture was team-oriented and collaborative. This individual was highly competitive and seemed to take offense at sharing customer information. Within three months, we knew that we had made a mistake and terminated the relationship. Although he did not succeed at our firm, he was still a successful sales manager and thrived in large competitive environments.

After conducting his exit interview we found that he did not adequately assess his work culture needs and accepted the first offer he received, which was from our firm. As a team oriented culture, we did not reward individual achievement but focused on those individuals that worked together, shared information, and found satisfaction by working in a team environment.

Avoid this mistake by taking the time to understand your strengths and your preferences for a work environment. Find your notebook and start answering these questions honestly and thoroughly.

1. What are your strengths?

Start your search by assessing the attributes that you feel bring the greatest value to a potential employer. As you analyze your strengths, make sure you consider those specific talents that set you apart from others. What makes you truly unique? Consider what you do better than your peers do. In addition, you need to be able to describe and illustrate your strengths to an interviewer. Examples might include: team-orientation, ability to multi-task, strong communication skills, web design, delegation ability, or motivational leadership. Why are you a better job candidate than your best friend?

Insider's Tip: Working with a professional career counselor can be beneficial if you are unsure of your strengths and preferences. Self-assessments can help you understand your personality preferences, career interests, values and skills. Visit our website for links.

2. In what type of work culture will you thrive?

Culture can be defined as the values, ideas, customs, skills, and interests of a people or group that are transferred, communicated, or passed along through the traditions and norms of an organization. As you consider culture, you need to truly understand an organization's values. What set of beliefs drives the organization? Because organizational culture is often hard to define, you should consider what values are most important to you.

For instance, are you interested in working for a company that believes that people are the most important asset of an organization, or a company that values the customer as the most important asset? In addition, you might consider the following examples, which should help you further explore the type of culture that interests you most.

Autonomy and independence vs. team collaboration

Do you value a structured environment, or do you feel that too much structure is restrictive and intrusive? Do you prefer to work in a group or team to accomplish a task, or do you prefer individual tasks and projects?

Work-life balance

Are you interested in finding an organization that focuses its efforts on establishing a healthy work-life balance? Are you interested in a flexible culture that focuses on intrinsic rewards as a method of motivating its employees such as time off, flexible work schedules, and telecommuting?

3. Where do you want to live now and in the future?

As part of a careful job search strategy, you need to consider all aspects of your life, including geographic location. Do you want to remain close to family and current friends? Are you interested in international assignments as part of your work? Are you interested in living near a large city? You must consider these questions as a way to narrow your company criteria during your search.

4. What type of company would you like to work for?

Are you interested in working for a private or public organization? Are you interested in a specific industry, such as information technology, financial services, insurance, or manufacturing? Are you interested in working for an international organization? Are you interested in finding an organization that has been selected as a "Best Place to Work" by national publications? Do you see yourself in the corporate world or in a start-up?

5. What kind of problems do you want to solve?

After all, employees are paid to solve problems. Do you want to solve problems with people, data, things, or ideas? Do you prefer to work with spreadsheets, teams, or technical instruments?

6. What types of positions are you interested in?

As you consider potential positions, look beyond just the title. You should specifically consider all aspects of a position, such as the skills, knowledge, experience, and education required. In addition, you should consider the following categories, which should help further define your ideal role:

Technical skills vs. functional skills

Are you interested in technical positions or functional positions?

Technical positions typically have a specific area of expertise and develop their role around the specific knowledge or content of the work performed. Functional positions are typically more general in focus and include a broad range of tasks. A functional position, such as an accounting specialist, can provide a very transferable set of skills that apply to multiple positions, whereas a tax accountant focuses on specific skills highlighting expertise.

Security and stability

Are you interested in a position that maintains a predictable workload? Are you interested in a specific position because of its stable role within the organization, such as an accountant versus a salesperson who relies on commissions?

Entrepreneurial inspiration

Are you interested in a position that provides the skills and knowledge that could help you develop your own business? Are you looking for a position that cultivates your creative imagination and allows you to develop new products or services? Are you looking for a position that provides creative challenges every day? Do you prefer an organization that values employees with an entrepreneurial mindset?

7. What type of manager motivates you?

Are you motivated by a manager who continually provides feedback or a boss who sets the direction and has a hands-off style? Are you motivated by a manager who leads by example and provides a lot of coaching? Are you interested in a manager who has connections and history with the organization? If you have not had much job experience, think about what kind of professors have motivated you. However, remember that in the working world, you will not receive as much feedback on your work and may not hear anything at all unless something is wrong.

8. Are you planning to continue your professional education?

Consider all educational goals that you would like to achieve, such as certified public accountant (CPA), professional human resources professional (PHR), or chartered financial analyst (CFA) certifications, or formal educational milestones such as an MBA or another type of master's degree. In addition, you should consider those organizations that support continuing education and have a training or tuition reimbursement program.

9. What are your long-term goals?

Where do you want to be in five or ten years? For example: "I want to be a partner in an auditing firm." "I want to be vice president of sales for an international software company." "I want to be chief financial officer for a manufacturing organization." "I want to work in a marketing organization where I can cross-train and learn from others." Whatever your long-term goals, you need to continually measure specific steps that help you get there. As you assess your career goals and target specific positions, you should also consider the types of organizations that could offer these types of roles, as well as the skills, knowledge, experience, and education needed for such positions.

10. What defines your company criteria?

We have included this step to help you develop a list of criteria that you feel is most important to you. As you implement your job search strategy, you should use the list you develop as your criteria in identifying those companies that you want to work for. These companies will be your target companies. Use the following list of attributes to help define your company criteria.

Financial stability   Public or private ownership

International   Technology focused

Strong client base   Strong leadership

Culturally stable   Strong employee orientation program

Chapter Checklist

✓ I've identified at least one short and one long-term goal

✓ I know what motivates me to work hard

✓ I can describe my ideal company, boss, and job environment

✓ I've identified my professional development needs

✓ I have determined key criteria for selecting companies

✓ I know why I am a better job candidate than my best friend

CHAPTER 3

WHERE DO YOU WANT TO WORK?

After discovering your core strengths and preferences and considering some possible occupations, you need to choose an industry in which to focus your job hunt. Then, you need to target **fifteen companies** and start a serious hunt. Don't just go knocking on any door.

A key strategy when preparing for your job search is to focus on particular firms in a particular industry. Limit the number of firms that you select for your research to no more than fifteen firms. This will allow you to spend time researching those firms thoroughly; you can gain an understanding of the firms' clients, products, services, markets, locations, and competition. If you select too many firms, you won't have enough time to really research those firms. And if there's one thing that we look for, it's a candidate who understands our firm, understands the type of position they're interviewing for, and most importantly, understands the types of products and services that we provide.

Before you can identify your top fifteen firms, you need to start thinking about what types of industries are of interest to you. First, let's consider your personal interests and the possible opportunities for various industries.

The first thing to consider when identifying an industry is your interest level and passion. Identify an industry where the products and services intrigue you, and you enjoy interacting with the type of clients common to that industry. Perhaps, you are impressed with the industry's public opinion or flattering reputation. Or the industry is exciting, like in the dot-com era when it was very exciting to be a part of the technical boom. At the time of this book's publication, the media was buzzing about alternative energy such as wind farms, solar development, and biofuels as well as opportunities in healthcare and senior living. Pinpoint your passion and then target industries that match it.

The second thing you need to think about when considering an industry is the possible opportunities for your career success. Maybe there is financial opportunity for you to make a lot of money. Maybe there is a historical trend within this industry that is interesting to you. Perhaps it has been around for a long time and you want to be a part of it, such as the manufacturing industry or the insurance industry, or the automobile industry.

Consider whether there is a geographic component to your industry. Are certain cities known for being technology hubs? For example, if you are interested in the software industry you might consider specific geographic markets such as Seattle, Washington; Austin, Texas; or the Silicon Valley. You will find firms that are in the technology and dot-com industries. Alternatively, you might be interested in overall domestic markets, or even the international market. If you are looking at an industry, for instance, or even the list of firms that you are going after, you really need to consider its geographic market. Is it a local-driven, local market? Is it a domestic market, or is it international? If you are interested in focusing on international opportunities and working for an international firm, then you really need to find the firm that operates in a global industry and has operations or aspirations to go overseas.

The third thing to consider is your own professional skills and attributes. What professional experience do you bring to the job? Do you have the skills and personality type to succeed in one particular industry more than another? For example, I currently work for a land development-consulting firm and many people within his firm have engineering backgrounds. Most of his colleagues have strong math and analytical skills. People with this analytical bent gravitate towards this industry, and they succeed in it. So take a good look at your skills and attributes and see if they match what is needed for the industry you are pursuing.

The fourth factor to consider is market conditions, which indicate industry growth and decline. At the time we wrote this book our nation was in a recession. While many companies and entire industries, such as the auto industry, were experiencing serious downsizing, other companies were growing. In any economy, urgent industries will appear on the horizon and provide opportunities for savvy job seekers who keep abreast of economic conditions and business opportunities. If you are interested in a product-based organization or a retailer, you need to think about consumer confidence. Do your research so you know whether an industry can survive an economic downturn or even thrive while other industries are suffering. Figure out if you are pursuing an industry that is recession proof or if it is very volatile.

There are many online resources available to conduct industry research. For example, www.Hoovers.com provides data on many companies. The *Occupational Outlook Handbook* www.bls.gov is regularly updated and can also provide information regarding the growth of various industries both on a state and national level.

Visit company websites and conduct **informational interviews** with employees to learn more about the industry outlook, the various competitors, and its national and global opportunities. Informational interviews are initial conversations with potential employers to learn more about the firm, the industry, and possibility of the specific positions within the firm. It is an informational process to get a foot in the door.

Attend **professional conferences and seminars**. Every industry has associations, conferences, seminars, and trade shows. For example, in the software industry in Chicago, there is an organization called the Chicago Software Association. Four hundred different organizations are members of the Chicago Software Association and are all linked by the Internet, and host a conference and tradeshow every year. These are the type of events that you should attend to network and learn more about possible job opportunities.

Finally, you can gain valuable information from your own **personal and professional network**. Ask friends and colleagues about the industry. Chances are somebody within your network works or knows someone who works within the industry that interests you. Maybe a parent or a friend is driving some of your interest because you think their job is interesting. Take the next step and speak with that person to gain occupational data. Ask tons of questions so you can understand the future of the industry, and the attributes that you need to successfully develop both as a candidate and as an employee.

From a long-term career perspective, it's very beneficial and easier to grow within an industry. If you carefully select an industry, you will develop knowledge and skills that pertain to that industry. For example, if we are looking to hire an accountant, our preference is to hire an accountant within our industry. These particular accountants will understand engineering software, products, and the types of clients that are in this industry. There are certain nuances of the industry that they will know from day one. We are more apt to hire an accountant from our industry than just a very good accountant.

Another example is if you're in sales and you want to transition to marketing or public relations, it is easier for you to grow from sales into marketing within the same company or within the same industry, than it will be to go from sales in one industry to sales in another. It is a difficult transition to change positions and industries all at once.

When you are identifying your preferred industry think about the long-term aspects of your career. When we are looking for candidates, there are three things that we look for that relate to industry success:

1. Skills and knowledge about the industry.

2. Education and experience within the industry or related to the industry.

3. Personality and cultural fit with the firm's culture.

For the long term, think about how any particular job opportunity will enhance your skills and knowledge. As you grow within an industry, your education and experience will continue to grow with certifications, continuing education credits, and professional development opportunities. Find an industry that intrigues you so that your interest will be sustained for your entire career. You need sustainable passion.

How do you choose an industry in a difficult economy? The key task is to understand market conditions and market drivers. In today's economy, you really need to think about what companies are going to be around for the next ten to fifteen years. During the past few years, we have witnessed many established companies come and go, especially in the financial industry. We cannot stress enough to job seekers to consider the market conditions in today's environment. Do your research so you know the rising and emerging industries that are actually investing, growing, adding new jobs, and receiving attention from consumers. Often referred to as **urgent industries**, these growing industries might be receiving tax incentives or stimulus dollars from the federal government.

A good example is the **alternative energy industry**. Renewable energy or alternative energy is receiving much attention, and for good reason. First, there are many tax incentives associated with investing in green technology and identifying areas that we can reduce our carbon footprint and develop green or clean energy. Keep your eyes open. You are going to see a significant amount of investment in wind farms, solar facilities, biofuel plants, and new innovative alternative power generation facilities.

Healthcare is also currently viewed as an urgent industry. Baby boomers are starting to retire and live longer creating greater demands on our healthcare system. There have been significant advances in medical technology and medical research, which is driving the longevity of our seniors thus requiring more services. And, because of their retirement, you will see a very large population utilize medical facilities, and put greater demands on pharmaceutical markets and health care manufacturing, which produces artificial limbs such as hip replacements. This is a hot industry right now as our populations grow, and the technology continues to advance while the pharmaceutical industry continues to conduct research and identify long-term opportunities. Other industry opportunities will open up in ancillary areas such as senior living, non-medical senior care, and even specialized transportation and other services for the elderly. Nursing, pharmaceutical sales, medical research, and biotechnology will offer employment opportunities for at least the next five to fifteen years.

Surprisingly, another industry that is starting to grow is **specialized manufacturing**. This growth is real despite the fact that manufacturing has become globalized and outsourcing and off-shoring have become common. America's innovation is starting to apply itself to very unique manufacturing such as hydrogen fuel cell batteries and solar panels.

Other industries that continue to remain stable include the **technical and service-oriented industries**. These types of jobs will continue to be required and these industries will continue to remain a sound growth sector for a long time. Plumbers, HVAC technicians, and electricians cannot be outsourced! In fact, most services cannot be off-shored, especially personal services such as therapists, funeral directors, or even cosmetologists.

Finally, you will continue to see career opportunities in **homeland security**. From greater security at your local airport to global opportunities, job growth will continue in this industry.

In short, you want to identify industries that align with your passion and interests and that provide both financial and growth opportunities. Find an industry that matches your skills and abilities. Choose an industry that is aligned with market conditions, so you can identify urgent industries. Then, you will be prepared for future career transitions because you will take that industry knowledge with you.

If you need assistance to jumpstart your thinking about industries, visit the Bureau of Labor Statistics website and view their *Career Guide to Industries*. You can search by industry and use the *Occupational Handbook* to view data about specific occupations. http://www.bls.gov/oco/cg/home.htm. After determining an industry, the next task of company research begins.

DETERMINE KEY COMPANY CRITERIA

As you develop your job search strategy, think about the types of companies for which you would like to work. You should develop a criteria list before you start your research. Many people place value on different aspects of an organization. Identify your most valued criteria and use it as a benchmark for your target companies. Below is a sample list of criteria that might help you establish your company criteria.

Stability: Is the company organizationally and financially stable? Does the company have a strong history and bright future?

Location: Is the company located where you want to live?

Quality products or services: Is the company recognized for superior output?

Cultural diversity: Is the culture welcoming of diversity?

Benefits: Does the company provide stock/profit-sharing program, group health insurance program, dental/vision insurance, life and accidental death insurance, short-term and long-term disability coverage, and paid holidays/vacation/sick days?

Clear organizational structure: Are there documented job descriptions and a clear process for promotions and transfers?

Career development: Does the company provide orientation and assimilation programs, educational benefits, documented feedback and performance evaluations and growth opportunities?

Work-life balance: Does the company share your views on balance and flexibility?

Collaboration and teamwork: Does the firm have a team environment or focus on individual accomplishment?

Company ethos: Does the company contribute to community organizations? Do you share the same type of social conscience? Does the company encourage volunteerism?

The next step is to identify **fifteen target companies** that match your company criteria. As you consider these companies, match each company to your list of important attributes. Is the location of the organization important to you? If so, your target companies might be in the same geographic region. Are you interested in a specific industry or specific company size? The most important aspect of this exercise is to force you to narrow your search to fifteen target companies. This exercise will help you focus on those companies that interest you.

Notice you haven't been asked if your target companies have open positions. At this point of your job search, identifying target companies that match your criteria is more important than looking only at those companies that are currently hiring. Industries change, job markets fluctuate, and companies' hiring schedules differ by month. As you begin researching companies, you might find that companies drop off the list, which will require you to add more names. In general, a better approach is to focus your time and energies on target companies that match your criteria than applying a shotgun approach to a job search, only to become frustrated very early in the process.

Identify the best resources to research the target companies

Start building your list of resources to research your fifteen target companies. These resources could be personal referrals from your network of contacts, corporate websites, career centers, trade journals, annual reports, and a multitude of free and for-pay company research tools on the Internet. Later in this book, we highlight multiple resources that you can use. However, for this assessment, we want you to identify those resources that you are currently aware of and to which you have access.

Determine the type of information you need

As you prepare to research each target company, develop a template to follow during your research. This template should highlight the most important information you need to gather during your job search. This assessment is the starting point, but as you read more of this book, this list of questions will grow. The following is a sample list of questions.

- What industry is the company in?
- How large is the company?
- Who are its competitors?
- What type of products/services does the company produce/provide?
- Who are the company's customers/prospects?
- What type of culture does the company promote?
- What type of benefits does the company promote?
- What criteria does the company look for when hiring?

Develop a plan to conduct your research

Now that you have developed a list of fifteen target companies, identified resources to conduct your company research, and developed your research template, you need to create a plan of action. As you begin, make sure to include organizational processes such as filing methods and written or electronic documentation of your findings. Your research needs to be easily accessible and understandable later in the process. You need to stay organized and focused on learning as much about each company as you can. This plan should also include a timeline and specific milestones to measure your success. How much time should you spend to research each target company? What is your timeline to find a job? What will be your weekly milestones of success during this search?

Insider's Tip: Many hiring managers and recruiters selected those candidates who did their research and understood the organization. Doing your homework pays off!

JOB SEARCH STRATEGY: TWENTY KEY QUESTIONS — AND YOUR BEST ANSWERS

These are questions to ask yourself. Sample answers are provided to give you an example of reasoned responses to key questions to keep your search moving in the right direction. Before you can answer an interviewer's questions, you must know the answers yourself.

1. What types of jobs motivate you?

   I am motivated by technology and am interested in a job where I can be creative as well as use my ability to work in a collaborative team environment.

2. Where do you want to live now and in the future?

   I want to stay in the Chicago area.

3. What type of job would make you happy?

   I am interested in a marketing role in a software development company.

4. What type of company would you like to work for?

   I want to work for an international software development company in Chicago that employs 1,000 or more people.

5. What type of starting salary are you expecting?

   My targeted salary expectation is between $35,000-$45,000 per year.

6. Are you planning to get an MBA, MS, or specific certifications?

   I want to find a firm that has a strong tuition reimbursement program that will help fund an MBA.

7. What type of company environment do you desire?

   I would like to work for a small private firm where I can wear many hats and learn about the business from various perspectives. I want to be a big fish in a small pond.

8. What type of boss/manager motivates you?

   I am motivated by a manager who is knowledgeable about the business and my role and will help coach and mentor me to reach my career goals.

9. Where do you want to be in five or ten years?

   I want to be a vice president of marketing in a software company.

10. What type of company would align with your career target?

    I need to work for a small software company that is market driven and has senior-level marketing support.

11. What type of education will you need to have?

    I need an MBA as well as professional certifications such as in Pragmatic Marketing.

12. What type of professional experience will you need to acquire to reach your career target?

    I need to acquire marketing experience in technology marketing, product marketing, company positioning, marketing communications, marketing research, and sales support.

13. Define your company criteria. What are the most important attributes of your target companies?

    I need to find a company that is market driven and provides an opportunity to learn and contribute. My target companies need to be software development companies in Chicago. My target companies need to provide a learning environment and focus on career development of their people.

    My target companies need to be team oriented and collaborative so that I can learn from others and provide feedback if needed. My target companies need to have strong software products that align with specific industries. My target companies need to be financially stable, have strong employment stability, and have a culture that supports diversity.

14. What type of company would have your target positions?

    Most software development companies that are members of the Chicago Software Association have marketing positions that are attractive to me.

15. Identify 15 companies that match your company criteria to begin your research.

    I have conducted some research for Chicago-based software development firms on Chicago Software Association's website (CSA.org) and found 15 target companies that match my criteria.

16. What resources should you use to conduct your research?

    I have a strong network in the marketing field and will make personal contact with professionals who can answer my questions. I plan to use the job boards such as Monster.com and Careerbuilder.com to a minimum and rely on professional organizations websites such as www.CSA.org and the Society for Information Management. Also, I will regularly visit the websites of my targeted 15 companies. I plan to use the Naperville Career Center to help with my search. I plan to contact each target firm to conduct an informational interview.

17. What information do you need to do your research?

    These questions need to be answered and documented as part of my research for each company.

    > *How large is the company?*
    > *Who are its competitors?*
    > *What type of products does the company produce/provide?*
    > *Who are the company's customers/prospects?*
    > *How do you define the target company's culture?*

18. How should you prioritize your target companies?

    I need to research each of these 15 and then prioritize those companies based on: My network's knowledge, open positions posted, and any past experience or competitive advantage I may have.

19. How much time should you spend to research each target company?

    I plan to spend one day just researching each company. I will develop a schedule for each day as well as document my findings based on the previous criteria that I have listed as important. I will identify specific milestones such as five interviews per week, five resumes and cover letters sent per day, and six hours per day spent researching target companies. I will provide my schedule to my wife to motivate me to stay on track and focus.

20. What is your timeline to find a job?

    My goal is to find a job in three to six months.

REAL-LIFE EXAMPLES: BEN VS. SUSAN

The more time you spend up front researching an organization and market data, the better the end results will be. Let us provide a real example. When we were recruiting for two open positions in our company, we found two similar candidates with the same educational background as well as the same type of work experience. One of the candidates was named Ben and the other was named Susan. Both candidates were well educated with bachelor degrees, extracurricular activities, backgrounds, and experiences. The position that they were interviewing for had an average salary range of $35,000 to $42,000. The small position posting on the Internet gave some company details and skill expectations as well as a starting salary of $35,000. The posting also had a link to our website, which provided more extensive knowledge about our company.

The first interview was with Ben. We asked him a series of standard interview questions such as, "Why should we hire you?" "What are your strengths and weaknesses?" and "What are your career goals and objectives?" Then we asked some very revealing questions such as "Tell us about our company." and "What are your salary expectations?"

Ben answered the standard questions very well, and we were very impressed. However, when it came to the specific questions about our company and salary expectations, Ben obviously did not do his homework. He told us that our company was in the software business and that we were international. These were fine answers that he read in the job posting. When we asked him if he visited our website, he said that he briefly reviewed the site but could not recall any specific information regarding our business model, office locations, or product line. We also asked him about his salary expectations, and he explained that the salary range posted was fine. Although we did not feel Ben spent much time researching our organization, we were impressed with his background and were planning to offer him the job.

When we interviewed the second candidate, Susan, we asked the same types of questions. Susan's answers were very good. We felt she was also very qualified for the job. When it came to the company and salary questions, Susan was much more prepared. She explained that our company had eight products and sold into four major industries. She told us that we were international with ten global offices, and she proceeded to list some of our customers in each industry. We could tell she did her homework.

When it came to the salary questions, Susan was also prepared. Her opening statement was, "Based on my research, I found that this position requires strong communication skills and technical knowledge as well as customer service experience. Based on these skills and the market value of the open position, which is $35,000 to $45,000, I am looking for a starting salary of $43,000 per year." Again, she mentioned that these figures were based on her research.

We hired both candidates. We paid Ben $35,000 and paid Susan $43,000. We are not suggesting that every company will match your salary requirements; she was right about the market value for the position, and we did not want to lose her as a candidate. From the very first day of employment, Susan's salary was at a much stronger position than Ben's because of her understanding of the market and her extensive research.

Make sure you spend time researching the company as well as the position's skill requirements and compensation figures. The job search process is like a sporting event. The person who has done the most planning, preparation, and practice has the best odds of success.

For your reference, in Chapter 10 we address conducting salary research and techniques, and negotiating your salary.

Chapter Checklist

✓ I have identified an industry which I am well suited for in terms of my interests, personality, and values and which meets my financial goals.

✓ I have determined the key characteristics of my target companies.

✓ I have identified resources to aid me in my search for creating my top 15 list.

✓ I have identified 15 companies that meet my criteria.

CHAPTER 4

WHAT INFORMATION DO YOU NEED?

Treat your job search just like a research paper. You first compiled data on yourself, then you've considered occupations and industries—but the research doesn't end there. Continue to do your homework and be resourceful, and you will make your own luck.

As you navigate through your job search process, it is important to be as resourceful as possible and identify all of the possible resources you can use to learn about opportunities. Research firms and network with those that can open career doors. You need to figure out what resources are available to you online, in your community, and through your network. Sometimes, the best resources are in your own backyard. Don't forget your alma mater; check in with your alumni association or college. Take a peek at our insider list of resources to find essential career information.

CAREER CENTERS (COMMUNITY OR UNIVERSITY)

Many universities as well as community centers offer career centers to help guide you through your job search. If you are currently a college student or recent graduate, the career center at your college or university is a great place to start. If you are not a college student, you should check with your local chamber of commerce or city hall to obtain information on local community career centers. Most towns have some sort of community career center that is available to residents. Even a local library could serve as a good starting point for conducting research. Career centers can offer a variety of resources to help point you in the right direction for your job search. One important tool that many career centers offer is an aptitude or compatibility assessment, which is basically a tool (similar to what you have just completed in the last chapter) that is designed to match up your interests with industries or job positions according to your personality or career goals.

There are many examples of personality profiles such as Predictive Index, Preview, Myers Briggs Type Indicator, and Strength Deployment Inventory (SDI). These tools can measure your abilities and aptitude, your behavior in different situations, your leadership abilities, or your personality traits.

Whatever tool you choose, remember that the results are simply data for you to consider. Do not rely entirely on these results. Use the results to better your understanding of your skills, abilities and traits and include them in your overall arsenal that you will use during your job search process. Often, these career assessments provide valuable descriptive language that you can use when articulating your strengths and abilities.

You can also use the results of these tools to help you identify what types of companies or industries you should consider targeting and researching. Most career centers have counselors available to assist you in this process or give career options. Once you have an idea of what industry or field that interests you and you have developed your target list of potential employers, you can take advantage of the multitude of informational resources available at the career center.

Whether contained in books or on electronic databases, resources at career centers should include:

- Industry information.
- Listings of companies within specific fields and where they are located.
- Salary guides such as Mercer, Watson Wyatt, or Culpepper. These guides typically segment the market by industry, position title, description, and geographic locations. Make sure the information is from a credible source.
- Industry outlook (for example, what industries are expected to need the most employees now and in the future). The *Occupational Outlook Handbook* provides accurate information.
- Financial information resources such as Hoovers.com, Dun and Bradstreet, or Leadership Library in order for you to conduct company research (what the company does, how they are doing financially, who their competitors are, etc.).
- Resume and cover letter information and examples.

- Professional career counselors to answer questions, teach interview and resume workshops, and provide private offices to conduct your phone interviews.
- Computer software programs available so you can complete a resume electronically.
- Database of current open positions you can search. In many cases, you can submit your resume electronically for positions that interest you.
- Contact list for various local companies or companies that frequent the center to recruit new hires.

Insider's Tip: When conducting company research, check to see when the company's fiscal year ends. Most companies have tight budgets at the end of a fiscal year but have an influx of budgetary monies in the early part of the fiscal year. Therefore, a good approach is to plan your job search for the early part of a company's fiscal year.

INTERNET

The most accessible research vehicle is the Internet. The Internet can be a very powerful tool if you know how and where to look for information. However, surfing all day is not a strategic approach and will not provide you with effective results. Instead, use the Internet like any other resource: with forethought and planning.

Focus on company websites

Once you have identified companies that you think match your career goals, the best place to start is the website for the individual company. These sites generally contain basic information about the company, such as what it does, what products it sells or makes, how long it has been in business, and where it is located. The sites may also contain information on the broader industry and the company's ranking within the industry (if applicable). Publicly traded companies usually have an investor relations section that provides financial information on the company. If they don't, you can look this information up on the Edgar database on the SEC's website (www.sec.gov), which focuses on public companies. Other information on a company's website probably includes press releases, customer testimonials, or other marketing information. Most companies post open job positions and will require you to apply directly via their websites.

Navigate through your target company's website and study sections that highlight the firm's culture, leadership, mission, history, products, and services. In addition, research their posted jobs on their site. Print off their position descriptions for the jobs that interest you and study the attributes that they are looking for. This information is vital during your resume development and interview preparation. Take their key attributes and description requirements and make sure your resume reflects some of the skills, experiences, personality and cultural fit items listed in the posting. In addition, start comparing the position descriptions from each of your target firms and identify overall trends, key requirements and desired traits of your targeted positions.

Search on industry-specific job boards, such as software and technology, manufacturing, retail, and nursing. In addition, some sites are geographically focused, posting jobs only for specific areas such as the East Coast or Chicago.

Insiders' Tip: If you are concerned with having too much information about yourself out on public display, there are ways to keep some privacy when posting your resume. If you are concerned about a current employer seeing your resume on a job board, don't list your company. Instead, just give the description of the firm. For instance, instead of saying "ABC Corporation," say, "A Fortune 500 software development firm with sales in excess of $1 billion." Make sure your email address is personal and confidential. Never use your work email address!

PROFESSIONAL ASSOCIATION/ORGANIZATION WEBSITES

Beyond the target companies websites, job boards, and search engines, we highly recommend visiting sites focused on professional associations and organizations. These websites often contain valuable industry information such as articles or newsletters as well as potential employment opportunities.

Many other resources are available online to assist you in your career endeavors. Check out these types of sites for online job listings specific to a target city or state. Local government sites or chambers of commerce tend to have websites that may have links to open positions within the community as well.

Search engines can also lead you to other valuable information such as salary guides or cost of living comparisons. These types of sites can be very helpful when considering a job for which you would be relocating to another part of the country. The key to successfully navigating your way through the Internet is to be creative, patient, and relentless.

PROFESSIONAL ORGANIZATIONS

Involvement in professional organizations or associations is another resource for your career development. If you are already a member of a professional organization, we recommend becoming involved in round-table discussions and events, committees, task forces, and monthly networking events. These places are all great for meeting people and networking with like-minded individuals.

If you are not involved with any professional organizations, get involved. Locate an industry organization that best suits you and apply for membership. Once you are a member, become active. You can network and socialize while you learn more about your industry and chosen profession. Moreover, you will be well-positioned to learn about open positions, meet hiring managers, and investigate companies or organizations.

Here are examples of professional organizations:

- American Accounting Association (AAA)
- Beta Alpha Psi
- American Marketing Association

- Society for Human Resource Management (SHRM)
- Toastmasters International
- Delta Sigma Pi
- American Council of Engineering Companies (ACEC)

Insider's Tip: If you are a student, run—don't walk—to your nearest laptop and sign up now for a student membership to your professional organization! The cost difference can be $30 for a student membership versus $250 for a non-student/professional, and the membership transfers with you after graduation.

PROFESSIONAL RECRUITING FIRMS

If you have been working for five or more years, you should begin to add professional recruiters into your job search strategy. Until you have five years of work experience, most qualified and reputable recruiting firms will not consider you as a truly viable candidate. Before jumping into the details and guidelines for working with recruiting firms, let us make this important point:

Spend no more than ten percent of your total job search time with recruiters. Do not fall into a common trap in thinking that you have a great recruiter who is going to find a job for you.

Recruiters do not make money by finding you a job. They earn their money by finding specific people for their clients—the company or organization that hires them to do this work.

Let's start with a brief overview. The two different types of professional recruiting firms are **contingency** and **retained**. (Knowing this
fact is not going to modify your approach, but we want you to look well
informed as you begin to approach these professionals.)

Contingency recruiting firms are paid only when their client (company) hires someone whom the recruiter brings. Retained search firms are
paid to be the exclusive search firm for a specific position. The assump-
tion is that they will work on the search until they find a person who
pleases the client. It most situations, retained search firms are typically
used for senior-level positions, those with salary ranges from $100,000
and up. From a networking perspective, we would encourage you to
spend some time taking several steps to maximize your reach within
this segment of your total network.

First, conduct some research to identify a list of recruiting firms that
you want to know you. Just like your search for target employer prospects, doing some upfront work can pay off handsomely in the end.

Find firms that specialize in your profession. Some firms focus on
just accounting or information technology. Make sure you are targeting
those firms that handle the career track you want to pursue.

Find firms that have strong visibility in your city or in the nation if
you are open to relocation. Once you have assembled your list of these
firms, the next step is to contact each firm with the following objectives
in mind:

- Confirm that this firm is interested in having you in its database. Do your best to ascertain that it has had business and is continuing to have business placing people like yourself.
- Ask if someone would be interested in meeting with you in person. If the firm is open to this, we believe it is a good sign that the company will do a better job in representing you and working for its clients.

Whether in person or over the phone, spend some time with people in the firm. You want to make sure that a few key things happen:

- Your resume gets into their database.
- All the contact information about yourself is entered correctly.
- They understand the specific types of jobs you are interested in and qualified for.

Depending on your experience and capabilities, a variety of positions might be appropriate. Most sophisticated databases can handle a person with multiple job preferences, but you need to make sure that the people entering your information into the database understand this. Some newer database systems allow you to enter your own information via the Internet. The advantage here is that you can tailor your profile exactly the way you want and ensure that your multiple job positions are accurately represented.

Finally, take some time to chat with the people in these firms and ask about the market conditions; what's hot and what's not? What companies are hiring? What types of positions are being filled? You can learn a lot about the current hiring climate from professionals who make their living finding people for companies who are paying significant sums of money to hire new employees.

Ask them to critique your resume. Again, you are on the phone or having coffee with people who earn their living reading resumes, interviewing people, and making decisions on whom to present to their clients based on those two activities. They truly are professionals in an arena where you need help. So, while you have their attention, benefit from their experience and opinions.

Thank them for their time and keep in touch with those whom you felt were truly professional and personable. Even after you find your next job, remember that your job-hunting days will come again.

Now that you've identified quality recruiting firms that focus on the same positions and industries as yourself—and you've taken the time to meet them, get into their databases, and listen to their suggestions— you can put that part of your job search on the back burner. Remember, only ten percent of your job search time should be spent with recruiters.

Following the steps we've suggested has put you ahead of ninety percent of the rest of the job hunters in the eyes and databases of professional recruiters. If you want to put yourself ahead of ninety-nine percent of the job hunters in the recruiters' world, take the step that will dramatically improve your networking results: Ask how you can help them!

You probably know someone in your network who would like to be linked to a very good, prequalified professional recruiting firm. If you've already done the legwork, research, and qualification, then you have a valuable piece of information that you should use. Bring together someone in your network with the best recruiting firm or recruiter that you have now uncovered. We can guarantee that taking this step will put you ahead of ninety-nine percent of the other candidates in that recruiter's list. Helping others who you would like help from always increases your chances of success.

Insider's Tip: For those of you with fewer than five years of work experience, begin networking with recruiters in your field. Learn more about their firm, their clients and their research. However, do not rely too much on leveraging their opportunities. Companies sometimes engage the services of contingency firms to conduct searches that may include entry-level candidates, but these types of searches are rare. If a recruiting firm contacts you, you should follow through and present your abilities, background and resume for their database. After you gain more experience and your compensation levels rise, recruiters will start showing interest and engaging you in their searches.

STAFFING AND TEMPORARY FIRMS

Although many job seekers might consider this a last resort, understanding this segment of the world of business and how to work effectively within it is becoming increasingly important in any good job campaign. Whether the company is called a temporary personnel firm, a staffing firm, or a contracting firm, with all of them you are legally employed by that firm and will be working at a client's office for that firm. The largest temporary / staffing firms include:

- Kelly Services
- Office Team
- Spherion
- Accountemps
- Manpower
- Robert Half
- Adecco
- Randstad
- Allegis

The most common category of temporary workers is administrative and clerical support occupations. However, professionals, including engineering, managerial, and technology professionals, now make up over eleven percent of the personnel supply services industry. Growth in demand for these skilled occupations is expected to outpace the growth in demand for temporary clerical positions.

Let's explain why a company would choose to hire a staffing firm to bring people to them, instead of just hiring the people directly. Perhaps it only needs the help for a project or a period of time. Many times companies have projects that have a specific beginning and ending date. Hiring a new full-time employee would not make sense, so the firm engages the services of a staffing firm to provide that specific talent for that specific length of time.

In addition, a company might have extra work because of an employee being on a medical leave or just unable to do their normal job, again creating the need for some specific help for a period of time. The company needs something accomplished, and it lacks specific expertise. A new computer system is being installed, a new product is ready for market, or employees need to be trained on some new systems or tools.

The reasons are many, but the solution is common. "Bring in someone who can help us get over this hump!"

The company is not sure they really need a new full-time person, so it hires a temporary worker first. As companies grow, they often feel the need to increase the employee head count. Bringing on new employees first as contract employee's can allow the company to test drive the person's abilities and allow the company to better understand the impact on the business. In this way, the company can determine if the increase in head count is the right solution while providing a way for the company to determine how well that new person fits into its environment.

Now that you have a better understanding of why companies use staffing firms and temporary employees, you can see how working with these firms can increase your pathways to success in your job campaign. Companies need people, just not always people that they employ. The image of temporary workers doing repetitive, low-skilled work is as outdated as black-and-white television. So, if you feel as though joining the ranks of the temporary workforce is beneath you, you are missing out on a huge segment of the future workforce. Whether you are directly out of college or have thirty years of work experience, joining companies in this method can be just as profitable and rewarding as being a full-time employee.

As with all the other aspects of your job search campaign, working for a staffing firm also starts with **research**. You need to find the staffing firms in your niche that focus on the type of work you are seeking. If you are a recent graduate and looking for an entry-level accounting, marketing, or advertising job, there are staffing firms that specialize in these categories. In fact, for those of you who are still unsure about your career plans, landing a position with a staffing firm may be just the ticket for exploring different types of industries and careers. We have seen several firms hire people fresh from college to handle very responsible positions that involved helping major corporations roll out new systems or introduce new products. These types of projects can involve a variety of responsibilities, heavy travel, and high visibility within the corporate headquarters. What a great way to start your career!

If you are well into your career and looking to make a change or are forced to make a change, staffing or contract opportunities are a great way to bridge the gap between those stages in your career. Find staffing firms that work with experienced people in your industry.

Regardless of your profession, temporary staffing is a viable and growing segment of our workforce. Find those staffing or contracting firms that deal with people like you. Introduce yourself to them, just like you would to a recruiting firm. Whether over the phone or in person, make sure they know who you are, what abilities you have, and what you can do. Make sure your resume is in their databases. Are you willing to travel? Are you willing to work forty hours a week? What is your desired hourly wage? As with your favorite recruiters, keep in touch and follow the Golden Rule! Maybe someone in your network could benefit from being linked to a pre-qualified staffing or contracting company. Connecting your preferred staffing or contracting professional to a new potential customer puts you ahead of 99 percent of the other potential candidates in that professional's database.

PRINT MEDIA

Another resource you can use for your research is print media: newspapers, magazines, and journals. In some industries, newspaper employment advertisements are still a popular method that employers use to find prospective candidates.

Most of these publications provide online editions making searching, researching and targeting firms easier. There are also tools such as Google Alerts that can notify you each time your target firm appears on the Internet.

As part of your search, you should review your local newspaper or the newspaper in the geographic area you are targeting and review the employment advertisements. In addition, review the stories in the newspaper regarding your target companies. Understanding the most current events regarding your target companies might be very useful.

Magazines are also very useful for company research. Some magazines target specific industries while other magazines focus on private companies or public companies. There are magazines that list the "Best Places to Work," "The Most Family-Friendly Work Environment," or "Employers of Choice." Some magazines have the top 100 or 500 companies in America for both private and public industry. Review these magazines to learn more about the companies you are targeting.

Chapter Checklist

✓ I have identified online and print resources to find the information I need.

✓ I have identified resources to help me with my job searching skills such as resume critiquing and mock interviewing.

✓ I have explored temporary work opportunities and professional recruiters.

CHAPTER 5

WHO DO YOU KNOW? WHO KNOWS YOU?

The people you least expect to help you in a job search may be your biggest advocates, so nurture all of your connections. Work your network virtually and in real time all the time. Connect with professional colleagues who can introduce you to potential employers and mentors. Nearly seventy percent of all job acquisitions begin with networking. Join this group of savvy job seekers who know how to secure a job. Read this chapter to learn how you can make networking work for you.

Networking often refers to a social activity typically utilizing reciprocal relationships to facilitate communication between people. Simply put, networking is leveraging all of your relationships in ways that benefit you and the other person. It's not just about what you get out of the relationship. It's about providing value to each and every person who crosses your path. Maybe you can't offer someone a job lead, but you can recommend a great recruiter or even a great salesperson in the suit department. Sharing valuable information is networking. While for some people, networking comes naturally; others need some help. Follow these networking steps for success:

Step 1: Make a list of all of your personal contacts that you may need to leverage during the job search. Include your peers, professors, college friends, parents, brothers, sisters, roommates, or anyone who might be able to give you a tip about a company, a job, or some connection associated with the company. Make sure this list includes contact information such as phone numbers, email addresses, and other relevant information.

Step 2: Segment your personal network list into subgroups such as school, work, church, professional organizations, and social organizations. A good way to do this is to have each contact listed on a three-by-five-inch index card, in an electronic database, or use MS Outlook to organize your contacts.

Step 3: Know what to say. Don't make blanket requests for help. They can be overwhelming. Ask for something finite and specific instead. Develop a script for each segment in your network, highlighting what you plan to say during the conversation. In writing the different scripts, consider the type of job you are looking for and the types of companies you are interested in.

Example: "Hello, John, during our conversation last week, you mentioned that you knew a friend at XYZ Company who was looking for a product manager for the Midwest division. Currently, I am looking for a new job and would be very interested in learning more about that opportunity. In fact, in my last position, I was the product manager for DEF product line, which is XYZ's largest competitor. Could I reference you when I call your friend? Thanks for your help."

Example: "Hello, Sue, last Sunday after church you mentioned that you knew of a career networking group that met at church every Saturday morning. As you know, I am looking for a new job in the field of marketing and would be very interested in attending with you. Would that be okay? Thanks, and I will see you on Saturday."

Step 4: Develop a game plan to contact your network via letter, email, phone call, and/or meeting. Within this plan, you might consider developing a message or announcement that could be sent to your network. We recommend contacting your network first with your message and then sending them a copy of your resume if they are interested. Your network has a network that has a network of people that have common interests. One often hears that we are all connected by only six degrees of separation. You never know who and where you might find your next lead. Use this plan to help communicate your efforts and goals of your job search to your broad network of contacts. Your list of goals to begin your networking should resemble the following:

- Finalize my resume and cover letter within a week.
- Develop a letter that informs my personal network of my intention to find a new job as well as highlights some of my skills and attributes.
- Distribute an email to my close personal network.
- Send a finalized resume and cover letter to people who show interest.
- Call and schedule lunch with my top five business colleagues.

- Acquire the schedule for the professional association's next networking event and schedule time to attend.

Once you have compiled your personal network list, begin to make contact (by phone, email, etc.) and see what names or contacts your personal network can provide. It is always a good strategy to have your friend, family member, or person on your network list. Call potential contacts at your target firms first if possible and if they are willing. Don't forget to leverage LinkedIn and ask for introductions via your network to professionals at target companies. The personal touch adds credibility to you and their referral.

As you gather networking names, create a **contact spreadsheet** with the person's name, phone number, occupation, and any other important information you may need to use later—especially the person who gave you the contact name. Make sure you also record personal data such as number of children, hometown, favorite sports teams, and so on. This is the type of information that can help you better connect to the person and remember personal details. You may contact these names years later and find out that some may be in a position to hire you.

An important component of networking is attending functions where professionals in your field will be in attendance and/or giving a presentation (trade shows, industry conferences, meetings, and small-group gatherings). These forums offer good opportunities to establish a contact in an organization and to learn more about the company, what it does, and its prospects for the future. Try to meet the speaker personally if possible. For instance, if a representative of a company is giving a speech, try to approach the speaker afterwards and discuss the speech, the company, or common interests. Be sure to introduce yourself and get the person's business card if you can.

When networking, the objective is to become connected and known to the people who have hiring authority.

Insiders' Tip: When networking for career purposes, identify your strengths and the value you have to offer. Convert those strengths into a value that you would offer a company or employer. In every interview, we ask, "What can you do for us?" You need to identify the value that you bring and phrase it in terms of return on investment (ROI). If the company invests in you, what benefit will it receive in return? Identify the types of opportunities you are targeting. Match your strengths to these types of opportunities or positions. While industry-specific organizations are more likely to produce job opportunities in your chosen career field, you never know where you might hear about open positions through community or religious organizations.

COLLEGE AND UNIVERSITY NETWORKING EVENTS

Many alumni associations host networking events to support job-seeking graduates. Check with your university to learn more.

If you are attending a large event, make sure you develop a game plan to cover all the ground efficiently. Identify the list of attendees whom you want to meet, including potential times and locations. Ask your personal network for recommendations on whom you should consider meeting. If possible, do some homework on the company and/or specific contact. In some cases, it may be appropriate to email or phone your contact or scheduled speakers in advance of the event. Mention that you'll be attending and looking forward to introducing yourself.

Track your progress. Make sure you measure your networking success by the number of meaningful conversations you've had. Make sure you focus on the conversation and the people you are meeting, not just the fact that you are looking for a job. Make sure you understand your contact's needs so you can understand how you can be of value.

Develop a list of intelligent questions: What type of projects are you currently working on? Is there any need for help with this specific project? Are you are looking to hire people with any specific skills? I noticed from my research that your company was merging with XYZ; how will that affect the projects you are tasked with?

What resources or ideas are you looking for at this event? If you are not a fit for that company's needs, you may want to provide a referral of someone from your personal network. Remember your **marketing theme** and match it to the contact's needs. You want to be in a place to position yourself as the answer to the needs of your targeted companies. For instance, "In my most recent position, we had to solve the same problem. In fact, my role was to . . ." Continue to build your network. Make sure you capitalize on the opportunity to ask for a business card and/or permission to make contact again soon.

Be very conscious of nonverbal behavior. If they are looking at their watch or looking around the room, use that time to say, "I do not want to take too much of your time. Could I get your business card and maybe we can finish our discussion after the conference?"

BUSINESS CARDS

There is a standard etiquette to receiving a business card. When someone hands you his or her card, make sure you read the person's name aloud. People always like hearing their own name, and it shows that you have interest and appreciate their card.

Then, once they leave, turn the card over and write specific characteristics about the meeting or conversation on the back of the card. You should document appearance, such as "blond hair, tall, black coat" to help refresh your memory. You should also document some facts about the conversation. For instance, "Talked about the Cleveland Indians" or "Found out that they will be converting their systems and need a project manager." The point of this exercise is to provide a refresher so that you will remember the person three months from now.

On our desks at our office, we have plastic index-card holders with business cards taped to index cards. On every card is a description of the person as well as their role and details about our last conversation. We have segmented the cards by industry as well as job function. We use this manual network filing system on a monthly basis to stay in touch with our close contacts. This process can also be automated with the use of a personal electronic address or contact tool.

We have a few final thoughts on networking: Smile, be personable, look people in the eye, and show your interest by asking questions and (most importantly) listening to their responses. Help others solve their problems or meet other contacts so that they will want to help you when the time comes. Networking is a reciprocal relationship. The more you care about others, the more you will succeed.

PREPARE YOUR THIRTY-SECOND COMMERCIAL

Successful networkers are always prepared to deliver their professional pitch or thirty-second commercial. Whether you use this pitch at a job fair, when you meet a VIP, or to answer the "Tell me about yourself" interview question, it is a helpful tool to have ready at all times.

Here's a sample script for a job seeker with experience: "As a sales rep for Tech Systems, I focused on industry knowledge, developing relationships, and growing revenue. My industry knowledge helped develop a list of forty qualified prospects. My relationship skills opened the doors to meet decision-makers and executive-level contacts and to identify potential solutions to their problems. In fact, the result is an average annual revenue increase of forty-eight percent over the past twelve months, at a time when the industry is experiencing a significant recession."

College students with less experience could answer like this: "As the communications coordinator for the solar car team at Michigan,

I wrote press releases, conducted interviews and wrote a blog. This experience has prepared me to work in the tech industry as a communications specialist."

INFORMATIONAL INTERVIEWS

Another effective networking tool is the informational interview. An informational interview is used primarily for two reasons: to gather more information about a company and to gather more information about industries or occupations. Whether you are just out of college or have fifteen years of experience, informational interviews are a valuable activity to provide clarity regarding your career choice and direction in conducting an effective job campaign.

An informational interview begins with a phone call to the prospective companies or people you have researched. Develop a script of the phone call before you call. The script should include everything you want to say to the company as well as blank sections for questions and answers you might discuss during the call. Make sure you study this script and know what you are going to say before your call.

Don't just read your script word for word. Nothing is worse than having someone recite a script to you on the phone. Just have a general idea of what you want to say and make sure the script is available as a reference. An example of this script appears on the following page.

The first person you contact will likely be the receptionist. He or she should be your first friend in the company. The receptionist is the initial gatekeeper and can play a large part in the hiring process. They are often asked questions about a candidate's phone etiquette and personality. Often, they are asked to give their general opinion of the applicants they speak with on the telephone and in person. Therefore, begin selling your skills to this person while gaining valuable information about the company. Make sure you learn his or her name and try to establish a rapport. Ask for the spelling of their name if you need it, and write down the person's name on your informational interview script.

Insider's Tip: The best way to start the conversation with the receptionist is to ask for help.

SCRIPT FOR COLD CALLING FOR AN INFORMATIONAL INTERVIEW

You: Hello, whom am I speaking with? My name is _____; I am currently attending Florida State University and am doing research on XYZ Corp. In this research, I am required to contact the accounting manager (or the department you are interested in). Could you please give me some guidance?

Receptionist: Sure, whom would you like to talk with?

You: I'm not sure. I would like to see if it is possible to schedule a fifteen-minute meeting with this person. Whom would you recommend?

Receptionist: I'm sorry; I am not allowed to provide names over the phone. I will just put you through to the accounting department. Is that okay?

You: Sure, Barbara. Thanks very much for your time.

Say the same thing to this coordinator in the accounting department as you did to the receptionist.

Asking for help and asking questions allows you to gather information as well as allow the coordinator to feel that he/she is important and helpful to you. Remember that the receptionist's role is to be a gatekeeper. Receptionists are required to screen every call and only let the important calls through. Make your call sound very important. If the receptionist does not put you through to the accounting manager, which is your final goal, the receptionist may want to take your name and have someone call you back. Give the receptionist your name and begin to ask more questions.

You: Would it be okay to send this person a letter? If so, to whom do I send it?

At this point, with any luck you can get the name and contact the person directly. If not, then explain to the receptionist exactly what your meeting is regarding. This step will be your final plea to get the accounting manager's name.

You: I understand, maybe you can help me. I'm graduating from Florida State University with a bachelor of arts in accounting.

> Because I'm very interested in working with you, I'm conducting research on your company. I just wanted to see if it would be possible to meet with someone in your accounting department to give me detailed information about your team. Is there anyone in your accounting department with whom I could talk?

They may put you through to someone in the accounting department or try to put you through to human resources or recruiting. When you are talking with the recruiter, give the same speech that you gave to the receptionist. One thing you will quickly learn in your career is that you need to have contingency or secondary plans prepared. Your goal is to put yourself in front of people who can help you. Whether you succeed with the recruiter or the accounting manager, any contact in a company is very important.

Another option is "Dialing for Names." This involves a phone, the main number at the company, and your guts.

Let us just say that the company's phone number is (555) 540-5000. Chances are that the company's extensions are also in the 5000s. Just begin dialing for names by dialing (555) 540-5001. When a person picks up, just politely explain that you must have dialed the wrong number and simply ask if they can transfer you to the accounting department.

Dialing for names does not always work, but give it a shot. You have nothing to lose.

Now, let's say you have been connected with the human resources manager or accounting department. Remember that this recruiter is only thinking about his current openings in the company and not your future at the company. Make sure you respect the person's time! Recruiters are very busy and tend to focus on their positions at hand. However, they know everything about the company and could help answer your questions if needed.

If you reach the accounting department, remember that they are also very busy. Reveal your interests in the company and your purpose for the phone call. They might ask you to send in a resume. Sure, send them a resume. You have done your research and you have seen the company's website. Try to build your resume around some of the company's values before you send it to the recruiter.

> **You:** "Hello, my name is_____. Do you have a moment to talk? I'm preparing to graduate from Florida State University in accounting and am beginning my job search process. I've done some research on XYZ Corp., and I am interested in learning more about your company. I'm conducting informational interviews with the companies in which I am interested and would be honored if I could schedule a fifteen-minute appointment with you to ask five questions about XYZ Corp. as well as the accounting and finance group."

Or,

"Hello Mr. Black, my name is Tim Augustine. Jim Butler gave me your name, and I would like to ask a favor of you. I'm interested in a career similar to yours. It would mean a lot to me if I could have the opportunity to meet with you in your office to ask some questions and maybe even get your advice regarding my career. If you are open to this, when could we schedule a meeting that would be convenient for you?"

The key to this interview is to build a business friendship. Remember that your goal is to gather information about the company. If you set up an informational interview with a recruiter or the accounting manager, make sure you utilize this time to gather as much data as you can.

After you contact each company and schedule an appointment, prepare a list of questions to ask. Make sure your questions are typed and convey the topics that are important to you in a company. Review your research and develop questions that will answer any questions that you have or were unable to uncover during your research. You should have five to ten detailed questions written out prior to the interview that will give you the best possible facts from which you will draw your final job decision. Here are a few examples of questions you could ask the person with whom you meet.

- What do you know now about this industry that you didn't know before you entered it?
- Would you have done anything differently?
- What types of characteristics are important for success in this field or with your company?

- What makes XYZ Firm different from its competitors?
- What type of special education or certification is required when working in this field?

When you are preparing for the interview, utilize the research you have already conducted. Read the company's annual report to gather pertinent information about the company's performance, products, locations, and so on. The purpose of the informational interview is to gather information about the company. However, the interviewer is also looking at your skills, knowledge, and dedication.

DRESS FOR SUCCESS

The next step of preparation is deciding what to wear. Your appearance for the informational interview is very important. (Refer to the "Dressing for Business" chapter within this book for clothing tips.)

YOUR PROFESSIONAL ATTITUDE

The final step of preparation is your attitude. Remember, you are just gathering information and building your network. Although you will be a little nervous, don't let the nerves get the best of you. You are not interviewing for a position; you are simply gathering data about a potential employer. The key to a successful informational interview is first getting in the door. You have already accomplished that. Now you should focus on gathering information and showing the interviewer that you are a responsible and dedicated prospective employee who is diligently researching the opportunities for employment.

You are already ahead of the game. Most job seekers are relying on their resume to get them in the door. As recruiters, we look for dedication and candidates who differentiate themselves among other job seekers. This technique of getting noticed is exactly that: a tool to differentiate you from John Doe job seeker.

During the interview, be yourself and smile. Remember that people are largely judged on appearance and attitude. Be personable, relax, and listen to every response. Make sure you ask specific questions. Also, make sure your questions are answered to your understanding. Remember that the interviewer is giving you his or her time and that you requested help. Be honest with the interviewer. He or she may turn out to be your best friend in the business.

A key rule for an informational interview is to learn more and *do not present your resume*. This may look like your informational interview is really a job interview and a way to get your foot in the door. Chances are, if your interview goes well, the interviewer will ask for your resume. Tell the interviewer that you are still in the research stage of the job research process. Let them know that it was not your intent to present your resume and that you sincerely appreciate his or her time and want to gather as much data as you can to make an educated decision.

We recommend purchasing business cards that have your name, address, phone number, and email address. Give the interviewer your card and ask if you can call in one week after your initial informational interviews. This step conveys that you are in demand and shows the interviewer that you are serious about your research.

Make sure you stick to your fifteen-minute appointment. Respect the interviewer's time. Be punctual. Arriving ten minutes before the scheduled appointment is sufficient. Think of everyone you talk with or meet as a prospective employer. Following the actual informational interview, make sure you follow up appropriately. The same day, no later than the day after the interview, send a handwritten thank-you card to everyone you met with. If you told the interviewer you would call in one week, make sure you keep that promise. Following up and staying in touch with your network throughout your job search is very important.

DEVELOP YOUR PROFESSIONAL IDENTITY

Whether you are looking for your first job out of college or transitioning careers, establishing your professional identity is an often-overlooked strategy. For some job seekers this is a very straightforward step. For example, if you graduated from nursing school, you know that it is important to join the American Nurses Association and maintain your professional continuing education credits. Likewise, many business professionals have an obvious professional organization that represents their interests and to which they belong. For example, human resource professionals belong to national, state, and local chapters of the Society for Human Resource Management (SHRM).

Liberal arts graduates, however, often have a harder time building their professional identity right after school because there is not a "society for history majors looking for well-paying entry-level jobs." After a thorough self-assessment, it is important for job seekers to determine what industries they want to work in. Once this decision is made, job seekers can move forward in getting involved in that industry on a professional level. For example, if you want to work in public relations, it is wise to join the Public Relations Society of America.

To research relevant associations please visit the Internet Public Library at: http://www.ipl.org/div/aon/. Websites of professional organizations can keep you abreast of recent developments, provide job listings, and offer career advice. Instead of looking at a generic job board, these job boards will cater to your niche market.

Insider's Tip: Don't just join the organization—engage in it! Attend meetings, or get involved in a committee where you will meet people, such as the membership or special events committees.

Establish relationships with professionals because these are the people who will someday be hiring someone like you. Give them the opportunity to see you at work so that they can vouch for your skills and enthusiasm for the profession. For example, if they see you "sell" the organization as a membership chair and increase the number of dues-paying members, and then they can recommend you for a sales position because they know your work ethic and sales skills first hand.

Remember, the people you meet in a professional organization can also offer you job shadowing and informational interview opportunities as well as refer you to job openings. These professionals are insiders. They work in the field you seek and they have the relationships and connections that you need.

Make sure the relationships you establish are not one-way. When we recommend engaging in the organization, the first step is to use your skills to benefit the organization first. Let them see you as a servant first, then a star, and then a colleague. Dazzle them with your talent and let them marvel at your contributions.

Another strategy to build your professional identity is to join local chambers of commerce where you will develop professional relationships. Joining civic service organizations will also build your stature in your community and help you extend your network of professional contacts. And don't forget your college alumni association, which may offer career services as well as networking opportunities.

BUILD YOUR PROFESSIONAL BRAND

Beyond building and maintaining your identity as a professional, to really get noticed you need to create a professional brand. While this may sound intimidating, it's all about differentiating yourself from the competition.

Think about a product as simple as ketchup. Do you buy the bargain brand or do you instinctively reach for the higher shelf brand? How was this brand marketed to you? Why did you first try it and why do you believe it is better than the generic brands. Nobody wants to buy something generic; we all want the best. Employers also want to hire employees that are top shelf so keep this in mind and review our recommended resources, which includes a book on personal branding.

WHO KNOWS YOU ONLINE?

The opportunities for social networking are growing exponentially, and we fear even naming some current products will date this book. However, we are compelled to give you some general advice.

Google yourself. What will employers learn about you from a search? Will they see photos that portray you as a dedicated professional? Will they see links to quotes you've made as an industry expert? Or will they see visions of collegiate escapades and read words you wish you hadn't spoken?

Even though you may think Facebook is just for your friends, employers are reading your profile too. Delete any photos that you would not want your mother or new CEO to see!

Use social networking to your advantage. Beyond posting a profile on LinkedIn, give and receive recommendations. Asking a professor to recommend you for your college work-study position or internship has credibility if it is on a reputable site. Post a professional photo and try to connect with as many people as you can. Ask business connections to forward your profile and connect you to other professionals in their network. Don't just post your profile, be a player and use the tools to your best advantage.

Chapter Checklist

✓ I have identified 100 contacts.

✓ I have a system for organizing my contacts.

✓ I have contacted thirty-five people and maintain regular contact with my top twenty people per month.

✓ I have written twenty notes.

✓ I joined a professional organization or community group.

✓ I attend professional and other networking events.

✓ I am involved in my alumni association.

✓ I know what a search of my name reveals online and it is professionally positive.

✓ I am actively using social networking tools to promote my professional brand.

CHAPTER 6

WHERE ARE YOU IN YOUR JOB SEARCH?

Take a few minutes to assess your progress. If necessary, write down your answers on a separate piece of paper.

1. Have you captured your internal assessment on paper? What are your unique skills, abilities and traits that you bring to a firm to add value?

2. What type of industry interests you?

3. What type of company interests you?

4. Have you identified your top ten target firms? (Who are they and why did you choose them?)

1.
2.
3.
4.
5.
6.
7.
8.
9.
10.

5. Have you compiled a list of resources to use during your job search quest? (List them here.)

6. Have you developed your list of personal and professional people in your network?

CHAPTER 7

SELLING YOURSELF

Think of your job search as a marketing campaign. The right resume and cover letter will generate interviews where you can verbally sell yourself. Now is the time to develop the perfect self-promotion pitch.

A critical tool in your marketing campaign is a strategically constructed **resume**, which adapts to every position for which you apply. Resumes are literally the tickets to interviews. As snapshots of your experience, education and abilities, they are written to convince employers to interview you. However, the resume development strategy that you develop should follow the initial steps of your internal assessment and your company research. This information will enable you to develop a more targeted and content rich resume by utilizing your initial steps of the job search.

This chapter illustrates a set of guidelines that lead to the development of a powerful resume and the other marketing pieces for your overall job search campaign. Design your resume with a word processing program such as Microsoft Word, which allows your resume to be emailed and viewed by most word processing programs. We recommend using various style formats such as bold, underline, and italics to make your resume attractive and pleasing to the eye.

If you do not wish to write your own resume, professional resume services are available at various prices. You can also check with you alumni association or local college career centers for personalized guidance or tools that can help you construct a resume online.

We do *not* recommend that you use a professional to write your resume because no one knows your strengths better than you do. And since each resume needs to be "righted" for each individual job, it would be costly to hire this task out. Instead, follow the advice in this chapter, and you will learn the essentials of effective resume writing.

APPEARANCE MATTERS

When giving or sending a hard copy of your resume, be sure to have your resume printed on high-quality paper. Good resume paper is a thicker, textured paper usually made of at least some cotton, which conveys a high-quality image. Use colored paper if possible because it stands out in a stack of resumes on a hiring manager's desk. Cream or light gray works best.

Preparing your resume to be distributed electronically is very important. Look at your resume on your computer screen and scrutinize it as you would on paper.

Be sure to email your resume to yourself. Does your resume appear organized? Does it read well on the screen? Use a hyperlink for your email address. (Microsoft Word's default settings turn your email address into a hyperlink for you.)

You may also want to consider more sophisticated programs such as Adobe Acrobat, which creates PDF files. A PDF will provide a very professional-looking document that will remain unchanged as it is emailed and posted electronically.

Keep the font size between 10 point and 12 point. Smaller font sizes are difficult to read, and larger font sizes indicate to the employer that you are just trying to fill up space. However, headings can be 14 point and make sure your name is the largest item on the page at 16 point.

The most important requirements for your resume are that it be neat and error-free. An error-free resume illustrates attention to detail and pride in your work. Remember, competition for most positions is very strong, and the slightest error could cost you the opportunity to prove yourself worthy.

Solicit the help of several people to review, edit, and provide feedback in an effort to increase the quality of your resume.

Insider's Tip: List dates of employment using years only if that is to your advantage. Do not lead with your dates. Lead with something that will sell you. Dates never will so we suggest that you place them at the end of the line near the right margin.

CONTENT MATTERS

Preparing a professional resume is a multi-stage process. You may want to create a **master resume** that lists all of your past accomplishments, responsibilities, and job positions. Make this resume as comprehensive as possible, because it will serve as a foundation for your final versions.

Organize your experience in reverse chronological order from present to past.

Keep refining this list as you go forward with the rest of the resume. Most people forget some of their accomplishments and responsibilities over time. This master document will serve as the foundation of every resume you write. Note, however, that you will pick and choose what information is most relevant to include on each and every resume.

As you grow in your career, you might find a need for multiple resumes that focus on different positions. You will list the same job titles and past employers, however, the way in which you sell your past experiences might require that you highlight specifics skills, experiences and abilities toward the different positions you may seek.

Should a resume be one or two full pages? That depends on the candidate and the content.

If you are a recent college grad with a few years of work experience, then your resume should be one page.

If you have enough relevant information (education, experience, and leadership skills that apply to the position) to fill up two full pages, then a two-page resume is fine.

A good rule to follow is that you can move to the second page after you have five years of experience or a graduate degree. If not, stick to a one-page resume. One page is fine if the information applies and offers a strong selling point for your skills.

Never have one-and-a-half pages of resume information. Use either one full page or two full pages. That piece of advice notwithstanding, remember that the information on the resume is important, not its length.

KEY SECTIONS OF THE RESUME

• *Contact Section* - Your personal letterhead.

The first section of your resume is the identification section and includes your contact information. At the top of your resume, you should insert your complete name in large bold letters. Using small caps is elegant, easy on the eyes, and will make your resume stand out.

The next step is to insert your complete address. Do not abbreviate anything. Fully spell out all words such as "Street," "West," "Colorado," and so on. If you wish to identify both a college or temporary address and a permanent address, place them on opposite sides of the paper. However, try to use only your current address or the address where the recruiters can find you today. This will give the impression that this version of your resume is the most current. Because your goal is to obtain an interview, they must be able to reach you.

Below your address, place your city, state, and zip code. Your telephone number(s), both daytime and evening, including your area code, goes below the address information. Make sure your email address is professional.

We do not recommend an email address like cubsrock1234@yourISP.edu for a professional resume.

If you are searching cross country for a job and don't want geography to limit your attractiveness, it is perfectly acceptable to list only your name, email address and phone number. This is also a way to increase privacy.

Letterhead Example

TIMOTHY J. AUGUSTINE

Campus Address
430 Lake Hall
Miami, Florida 44444
(555) 672-0000

Permanent Address
2434 West St.
Miami,   Florida 44444
(555) 929-1111

Tim@yourISP.edu

If you have only one address, place it in the middle of the page:

TIMOTHY J. AUGUSTINE

2434 EAST WHITE STREET, MIAMI, FLORIDA 44444

(555) 929-1111   Tim@yourISP.edu

Also, keep in mind that creating your personal letterhead, which you should also use on your cover letter and other written correspondence, is part of your personal branding. If you use a silly font, you may be sending the wrong message.

• *Objective or Summary?*

The next step is articulating your career objective. An objective that describes your goals to the employer should be short and to the point, yet fully illustrate your desire and your professionalism.

Remember that an employer has many resumes to review, and sometimes all they look at is your objective. Most companies receive an average of two hundred resumes for just one open position. The slightest error or a poorly written general objective statement could send your resume quickly to the circular file (the trash).

You don't want to leave the employer wondering what job you are seeking. Therefore, you need to make your objective statement eye-catching and to the point. Employers like to see objective statements that illustrate what you want to do for the company, not what you want the company to do for you. The objective reveals what you want to do, and the rest of the resume develops the reasons that qualify you to do it.

You may also use a summary in place of an objective statement. A summary is often preferable when the applicant has significant work experience. A summary statement uses three to five strong sentences that highlight your accomplishments and link them to your career goals. You can highlight leadership skills, expertise, or personal strengths. Avoid descriptions that can't be quantified or are generic such as "people person." Finally, use either an objective or a summary, never both!

Objective Resume Examples

OBJECTIVE

A position in medical supply sales that will give me the opportunity to use my medical background and communication skills to contribute to the success of the firm.

OBJECTIVE

An entry-level position in accounting with a global financial services firm.

OBJECTIVE

A challenging position that requires creativity and communication skills in the field of marketing.

Summary Examples

SUMMARY

Bachelor's degree and an MBA degree in marketing from Northwestern University. Excellent presentation and communication skills. Speak Italian and German. Experienced in all aspects of international marketing research.

SUMMARY

Bachelor's degree in financial management. Successfully completed an internship with XYZ Corporation in Cleveland, Ohio. Developed communication skills through Toastmasters International. President of student government and professional business fraternity.

SUMMARY

Global marketing executive with strong leadership experience in technology marketing, including company and product positioning, market segmentation definition, and analyst relations. Solid business foundation and experience in software sales and business development. Executive-level organizational leadership with well-rounded communication, presentation, teamwork, and Interpersonal skills.

These objectives and summaries are intended to offer a set of guidelines only. Many other ideas can also be very effective. Bounce ideas off other people during the editing process to create a resume that best reflects your talents and strengths.

Remember, it's all about what <u>you can offer the company, not what you hope to gain from the position</u>. Do not ever state that you want a position that will offer "opportunities for growth and development." The employer assumes you want to grow but they are hiring you to solve problems and grow their business. Keep in mind that they are focused on their bottom lines, not on employee development.

• *Education Section*

If you are currently a college student or a recent graduate, you should list your education after the objective statement. However, if you have more than five years of work experience, you should consider listing your professional work experience before your education to highlight experience beyond five years. Companies are much more interested in your experience that you bring to the position. If you have relevant work experience, make sure it stands out on your resume. The education should then follow.

If you have attended college, the company will assume that you graduated high school. Therefore, we do not recommend listing your high school experience in the education section.

List your most recent degree first, followed by the month and year of graduation. Also, list your college and its location. State your majors/minors and your GPA if it is greater than 3.0. If your GPA is lower than 3.0, you may not want to put it in writing. If it is not in writing, the interviewer may forget to ask.

If you lack relevant experience on your resume, short list your significant course work that is relevant to the position you seek and highlight other softer experiences you have such as teamwork, conflict management, and the ability to motivate others. List the classes you have excelled in and those that are pertinent to your major. Avoid introductory courses and only mention higher-level courses with impressive course names! However, try not to list more than four courses.

If you have significant work experience, place the education section after your work experience. Employers hire because of experience, but if you do not have a lot of experience, list education first.

Education Examples

EDUCATION

Bachelor of Science: May 2009

University of Michigan, Ann Arbor, Michigan

Major: Biology

GPA: 3.5

EDUCATION

Master of Business Administration: May 2011

Wharton School of Business, Philadelphia, PA

Concentration: Finance

GPA: 3.6

• *Professional Work Experience*

The next section is work experience. Any of a myriad of titles can head this section, but the best are very specific and will relate directly to the field in which you are seeking employment. For example:

Business Experience

Professional Experience

Internship

Finance Experience

Teaching Experience

Marketing Experience

Start listing your <u>most recent</u> experience. This is called reverse chronological order.

The first step is to list the company with a brief description, the title of the position you held and the dates in which you held the position. You should also include the employer's city but not address (see examples). Always provide a brief description of the firm where you worked. If it is a small firm, it will provide the recruiter with needed context of your background. If it is a well-known firm, it could boost the perception of your experience.

Marketing Experience Examples

ABC Software, Chicago, Illinois   *2009-Present*
International Software Company with operations in the United States, Europe, South America, and Asia, targeting industries including financial services, telecommunications, insurance, and retail.

Vice President of Global Marketing
- Senior-level business executive reporting directly to the chief executive officer.
- Held responsibility for worldwide market development activities, including category creation, company and product positioning, target market development, and revenue generation for new and existing software products and services.
- Developed a world-class marketing organization recognized by industry analysts.

- Designed and implemented the market development plan, which focused on company positioning, brand development, market research, market analysis, and product launch.

Marketing Specialist

- Member of a five-person global marketing team that implemented various marketing programs such as event planning, marketing communications, market research, and web design.
- Championed multiple customer and prospect industry forums, raised awareness of our company and products within our target markets of financial services, insurance, telecommunications, and retail.
- Developed and cultivated a customer advisory board that provided executive-level advice and direction regarding industry-specific solution development and customer relationship strategies.

Wording of Bullets

As you describe your experience and responsibilities, try to use phrases rather than entire sentences and eliminate all personal pronouns such as "I," "me," and "my."

You should use <u>strong action words</u> such as "achieved," "coordinated," and "designed" to describe what you accomplished.

Describe how well you did the job and explain your accomplishments during the experience. As you describe your experiences, focus on the tasks assigned, activities involved in completing the tasks, and the quantifiable results. Focus on developing a result-oriented resume that will show the recruiter your accomplishments and reveal that you are a results-oriented candidate.

Use nouns specifically related to your field. Employers—and the software often used to scan resumes—look for such keywords. For instance, include specific products, services, programs, or training such as Six Sigma. One example would be, "Conducted order entry of stocks, bonds, and mutual funds." Upon scanning this resume, the employer immediately notices that you are familiar with specific products used in that industry.

Include various programs or services you have used in school or previous jobs that might be applicable to an industry. For instance, you might indicate that you have conducted research using Dun and Bradstreet or Value Line.

This section of your resume is very important, and you should spend significant time getting it right. Be creative in your descriptions. Take everyday tasks and turn them into traits useful to the employer. For instance, avoid general job descriptions such as "clerical work," "filing," or "answering phones." Instead, depict these tasks as "office management, information organization and retrieval, and customer service operations."

Take each task you performed and illustrate how the experience has prepared you for other jobs. Be sure to use examples of experiences related to the job you want to obtain.

Quantify your information, such as, "increased revenue by 25 percent, reduced turnover by 10 percent, and managed a budget of $5.6M."

Too often, job seekers list every job they have had and what they did, just to have it written on the resume. A better approach is to understand the skills required for the position you are applying for and to emphasize those traits. For instance, if you worked for four years as a waitress/waiter but had a one-semester internship in the field of your choice, elaborate on the internship and be brief with the food service job description. This presentation emphasizes the experience that is directly related to your career goals, and downplays jobs you have taken just for the money. However, a waitress/waiter job is not without value because success in that position demonstrates solid communication, social, and customer service skills.

Use a variety of these <u>action verbs</u> in your resume. Always use present tense for bullets relating to a current position and past tense for a past position.

accomplished	achieved
acquired	administered
advised	appointed

How Hard Are You Knocking?

assessed	assisted
assured	brought
budgeted	championed
collaborated	communicated
composed	controlled
coordinated	delegated
demonstrated	developed
educated	encouraged
established	evaluated
expedited	formulated
fostered	implemented
initiated	led
maintained	motivated
negotiated	organized
persuaded	programmed
recommended	researched
reviewed	selected
strengthened	supervised

supported	targeted
transformed	tutored
facilitated	managed

Insider's Tip: Avoid having your resume read as if it is your job description. You must sell yourself in your resume, not list your responsibilities. Highlight your accomplishments, not duties! So avoid phrases such as "responsible for." Your bullets should not sound like you cut and pasted them from your job description. Instead, document what you achieved above and beyond the job description. What did you do that your colleagues neglected to achieve? Create bullet points with strong verbs that sell your achievements!

WORK AND RELATED EXPERIENCE EXAMPLES

SALES EXPERIENCE

Sales Executive. Gracelogic, 2010-present
- Managed business development and large-account selling software products and services within a geographic region. Focused sales activity within the financial services, tele-communications, and retail industries.
- Managed a comprehensive sales cycle, which consisted of prospecting, needs analysis, proof of concept, proposal,

billing, and collection with an average cycle time of six to nine months.

- Exceeded personal sales quota by 25 percent annually.

Account Executive, Hamburgerland Midwest Region, 2009-2010

- Developed key strategic customer partnerships with Hamburgerland's corporate and franchise stores as well as independent and national food distributors.
- Managed multiple sales cycles and product rollouts within Ohio, Michigan, Indiana, Pennsylvania, and Illinois.

Brand Manager, XYZ Cheese, 2008–2009

- Successfully implemented all promotions, trade support, financial tracking, competitive analysis, and new product development to including positioning, product development, packaging, pricing, marketing plan, and management of sell-in.
- Managed the XYZ Cheese business, including a $19 million advertising and promotion budget. Brand delivered volume, share, and record profit growth, reversing historical declines.
- Led breakthrough product introductions that grew grated cheese product volume by 12 percent.

Computer Tutor, University of Michigan Summer Institute, 2007

- Developed training classes for computer methods.
- Instructed classes of 15–20 students, focusing on Microsoft products.

- Served as a computer engineer for the computer lab and completed tasks such as updating existing systems and converting to a new platform.

The work experience section of a resume reveals to the employer what you can do as well as what you have accomplished. Make each point stand out in order to reveal your expertise and to illustrate your achievements in past jobs.

Consistency is the important key in this section. If you use bold-face type for your position in one instance, use it for your position every time. Notice the dates in the examples. They can be in either months or years. Years are preferable when you need to give the appearance of a longer work experience. During the interview, you will discuss the exact timing of past jobs, but this approach might propel you past the front door or past the gatekeeper reviewing the resumes. Remember to be honest, professional, and creative, and most importantly, pay attention to detail!

LEADERSHIP EXPERIENCE

This section of the resume illustrates leadership experience and extracurricular activities, both of which show energy, initiative, and interpersonal skills. NEVER use the word "volunteer," as it could be viewed as passive and may not sell your leadership or teamwork experience. You might consider using descriptors such as Campus Leadership or Community Leadership.

First, list the position(s) held and state the name of the organization. Also, include the location of the organization and indicate the time span of the position.

LEADERSHIP EXPERIENCE

Board of Directors, Naperville Career Center, 2008–2010

- Acted on behalf of the career center with organizational funding and scheduling of activities, as well as evaluating and implementing services provided to the community.

President, Alpha Chi Omega Leadership Board, University of Michigan, 2008-2009

- Planned monthly meetings and secured professional speakers.
- Followed Robert's Rules of Order and functioned as liaison between student body and faculty.

Vice President, Ski Club, Chicago, Illinois, 2008–2010

- Assisted the president with management of this eighty-member club.
- Planned trips to Denver and instructed new members on different techniques of skiing.

President, Delta Sigma Pi, Professional Business Fraternity at Polytechnic University, 2008–2010

- Formulated the structure for the 108-member Polytechnic chapter and all of its activities.

- Provided guidance and leadership to 12-person Leadership Board.
- Lead the chapter to receive Chapter of the Year award at Grand Chapter Congress.

• *The Honors Section*

After describing your leadership roles, follow with the honors section. List the activities in which you have received honors. In general, you will need to start with your collegiate achievements. One exception to this guideline is for candidates looking for a job in education. Future teachers can list their high school activities and honors. If you were your school's valedictorian, try to share this honor in another way by focusing on the scholarships you won due to this achievement.

HONORS

National Dean's List, 2010
Honor Roll, Delta Sigma Pi, 2010
Golden Key Award, 2009
Delegate of Kent State, Beta Pi Chapter, Delta Sigma Pi, 2010

• *Hobbies and Interests Section for a Resume*

Hobbies can only be included if they directly relate to your job search. For example, if you want to work for Zingerman's, a gourmet food company, you could mention that you are a chef even if the position you seek is marketing because the connection is relevant. Again, candidates in education can also include this section since they may be called to wear other hats in addition to a classroom assignment such as cheerleading coach. Listing camping is relevant if you want to work for REI or Eddie Bauer. Mentioning an interest in international travel could be helpful if a position requires international travel.

The purpose of this section is to give a better picture of who you are to an employer. The danger is that it can be meaningless and may not position you well. We highly suggest that you use the Community Leadership section to reveal your best qualities and experiences that may take place out of your professional domain.

• *References*

The final section is for references. It usually states that references can be provided if necessary. This section is considered optional. Employers often assume that references are available upon request. Therefore, omit this section if you wish to conserve space.

On the other hand, you may want to include on a separate page the actual list of references with your resume. In this case, you would simply list each reference's name, title, company, address, email address, and phone number. It is also helpful to describe your relationship to this reference such as former colleague, present supervisor, etc. If you do include references, list four to six contacts.

REFERENCES

Joe Smith jsmith@rotomola.com
Vice President of Manufacturing
Rotomola Corporation
Former Supervisor
123 Main Street
Chicago, IL 99999
(555) 456-7890

During your interview, you should always be prepared to present references. Have four to six references identified. You should include two professional references from people you have worked with in the past. You should have two peer references that include friends who could serve as a character reference. Finally, have two reference letters from either a professor or a manager.

Make sure you contact the references prior to providing their names to the recruiter. When you call them, ask for their permission to offer their names. Send them a recent copy of your resume. Tell them about the position you are considering. Share the job description with them. You should also let them know the expected timeframe of the call. Remember to make it as easy as possible for your colleagues to be your references. Follow up with them afterwards with a thank-you note or gift.

Insider's Tip: How do you provide a reference if you don't want your boss to know that you are considering leaving? Try to find someone you trust in the organization who has observed your work. Alternatively, someone who has left the organization who supervised you is always a good bet. Sometimes, a colleague can be a good reference when a supervisor is not required.

CONNECT THE DOTS WITH YOUR COVER LETTER

A cover letter is a simple document designed to introduce yourself, give a brief overview of your objectives and qualifications, and, most importantly, the value that you can bring to the company or organization. While your resume markets you as the best candidate for a given job, and the job posting describes the job, the cover letter can connect the dots between these two documents. A cover letter provides the opportunity for you to sell yourself as the most qualified candidate for any given position.

With the current trend of online applications and resume downloads, cover letters are not as crucial as they used to be. Often, an applicant will email a resume and just include a short email message.

However, there are times when a cover letter can be an effective marketing tool. A cover letter provides a clear example of writing ability and in many fields this is a critical skill. As you develop this letter, you need to answer three questions:

1. What problems does the potential employer have that need to be solved?
2. How can I highlight my strengths, and show in this introduction letter that I can help the employer?
3. How can I demonstrate the value that I can bring to the organization?

Rather than addressing the letter to "Dear Sir or Madam," the letter must be addressed to a specific person. Find out the name and title of the human resource director or the hiring manager.

The letter should be three to four paragraphs long and convey the value that you can provide as well as your interest in a specific position with the prospective firm.

The letter should be focused on the employers' needs instead of your wants. Your focus on the employer, rather than on yourself, always earns more attention, interest, and action.

The cover letter is segmented into three parts:

• *Introduction*

The introduction is a brief statement that mentions the position you are interested in and how you learned about it. Keep in mind that the recruiter or hiring manager reads many of these documents, so keep the introduction interesting and relevant.

Example:

> I am writing in response to an open sales manager position for the Chicago region. I learned of this opportunity through the Sales and Marketing Executives of Chicago, where I serve on the Board of Directors. Throughout my professional career, I have prided myself in continually proving my ability to build customer relationships, coach sales teams, and grow revenues.

• *Body*

The body of the cover letter is typically a one-or two-paragraph summary of your skills, knowledge, experience, and career goals. Focus this section on your understanding of the employer's needs, and match your strengths to those needs.

Example:

> Based on my knowledge of XYZ Company, I feel that the product line is competitive, the organizational reputation is strong, and the customer base is solid. The candidate you are looking for should be well versed in consultative selling and large account management, as well as provide a solid level of technical understanding needed to lead a sales team.

> As you can see from my enclosed resume, I have successfully performed at ABC Software for eight years, growing the business by 45 percent annually. Prior to joining ABC Software, I worked for X Software for twelve years, growing sales revenue annually and exceeding my quota of $2 million in sales of products and services per year. Through this work experience, I feel that I can quickly transfer my skills to help XYZ Company hit their regional goals of $5 million as stated in your annual report.

• *Conclusion*

The final paragraph is your chance to close the deal. Ask for the interview. Mention how you will follow up with the employer to set up a meeting.

Example:

> Given my skills in relationship selling, familiarity with the product line, and understanding of your clients' needs, I believe I could be of immediate value to XYZ Company. I would welcome the opportunity to meet with you to review my qualifications and to better understand your needs for the position. I will call you next week to set up an interview at your earliest convenience.

The following examples of resumes and cover letters apply the guidelines mentioned in this chapter. Analyze each of them. Take different ideas from them and build your own perfect resume and cover letter to best represent you to prospective employers.

Entry-Level Resume Example

JOB LOOKER
1000 OAK LANE
COLUMBUS, OHIO 44240
(555) 777-1000
Jobseeker@yourISP.edu

Objective

To obtain a human resources position with an organization where my training and development experience will contribute to workplace productivity and employee job satisfaction.

Education

Bachelor of Business Administration, April 2011

University of Michigan, Ann Arbor, MI

Major: Human Resources

GPA 3.5

Human Resource Management Experience

Center for Independent Living, Ann Arbor, MI

Internship, 2009-2011

- Developed employee training manual for 1000 employees
- Trained new employees on policies and procedures via lunch and learn and online applications
- Planned conference and training events for an average of 300 employees

The Uncommon Grill, Ypsilanti, MI

Server/ Trainer, 2008-present

- Established training programs for new employees resulting in 25 percent productivity increase.
- Developed promotional programs resulting in a 45 percent annual increase in sales.
- Managed monthly training programs for 25 associates focused on product knowledge.

Professional Organizations

Student Society for Human Resource Management (SSHRM)

Recognition Director, 2009-2010

- Formulated recognition programs for students' professional development in other organizations during their college career.

Delta Sigma Pi, Professional Business Fraternity

President, 2008-2010

- Formulated the structure for the 108-member Polytechnic chapter and all of its activities.
- Provided guidance and leadership to 12-person Leadership Board.
- Lead the chapter to receive Chapter of the Year award at Grand Chapter Congress.

How Hard Are You Knocking?

Honors/ Awards

Golden Rose Society Award

University of Michigan Orientation Leader Award

National Dean's List, 2010

Honor roll, Delta Sigma Pi, 2011

Mid-Level Resume Example - This resume is fine for a candidate with an MBA and nearly twenty years of experience.

EMILY B. A. MANAGER

430 MAIN STREET, PLEASANTON, CALIFORNIA 65588

555-255-4227

MBA@YOURISP.EDU

PROFESSIONAL SUMMARY

Experienced leader with an MBA and excellent project management, problem solving, analytical, and communication skills. Solid background in Fortune 100 telecommunications consulting and insurance marketing, product development, and operations. Proven success working in both team and independent environments.

PROFESSIONAL EXPERIENCE

Strategic Consulting, Chicago, IL, 2000–Present

A management consulting and technology services organization with more than $11 billion in annual revenue.

Consultant, Communications and High-Tech Market, 2007–present

Supervised teams of consultant and client personnel, created work plans, managed the timely completion of project deliverables, built and maintained strong client relationships, facilitated group discussions, reported team status to project senior management, documented system requirements, and mentored junior project members.

- Team Lead, CRM Project: Identified business and technical requirements, selected contract management software solution, and implemented this software for more than 25,000 customer service representatives. This initiative was part of a multiyear CRM program to transition a Fortune 100 telecommunications firm from a product to a customer focus.
- Created the User Acceptance Test (UAT) work plan, schedule, approach document, and scenario template.
- Coordinated UAT project test schedules and entry/exit criteria with the leaders of all other test teams.
- Supervised and directed the work of consultant and client personnel to collect technical requirements.
- Documented call center volume data and infrastructure cost information for the contract management software selection.
- Developed an inventory of the data elements to be used by the contract management software.
- Created statement of work documents to describe the function, data flow, and requirements of several incumbent computer systems that the contract management software would interface.

Business Analyst, Central Office Project, 2002-2007

- Evaluated client needs to design and implement a software application to manage technician workflow, work assignment, and time reporting. This application resided on a wireless handheld device, presented a standardized user interface, and managed legacy systems.

- Analyzed and assessed high-level project goals to produce business vision and project assessment documents.
- Created process flow and system documentation through site visits and subject-matter expert interviews.
- Co-led a requirements preparation team to create process templates.

Team Lead, Technician of the Future Project (CIO magazine CIO-100 award winner, May-August 2001

- Project team developed an enterprise-wide application for more than 30,000 field technicians of a Fortune 100 tele-communications firm to be used for job dispatch, trouble testing, material ordering, and time reporting. This application interfaced with numerous legacy systems, presented a single standardized platform, and was deployed on a durable laptop that used wireless technology.
- Trained and managed a team of consultant and client personnel to provide test data support to all project teams including development, product test, QA test, architecture, and infrastructure.
- Implemented several process improvements for system flow-through and test data in faster detection and correction of system defects.

Analyst, Communications and High-Tech Market, 2000–2002

- Developed problem-solving skills, gained knowledge of the telecommunications industry, ensured timely completion of project deliverables, reported status to team leadership, built and maintained strong client relationships, and produced process improvements.

- Championed the project team's knowledge building and test data coordination for the application's most critical and widely used legacy system.

- Developed contacts with client personnel, and leveraged relationships to solve complex issues.

Liberty Insurance Company, Livermore, **AR.** 1991–2000

A life and health insurance company with 300 employees and $188 million in assets.

Manager, Life Marketing, 1997–2000

- Managed the operational, product development, training, and administrative functions for the life line of business.

- Created and implemented plans to promote and protect profitability.

- Led a team during a nine-month project that developed an on-site, NASD-licensed broker-dealer branch office.

- Managed a 10-month project team that outsourced the premium billing, remittance, and broker-dealer functions to a third party administrator. This protected approximately $4 million in annualized premium.

- Solved problems and gave direction as the point person for approximately 40 people across departments including customer service, marketing, new underwriting, programming, accounting, and agent licensing.

Account Coordinator, Life Marketing, 1994–1997

- Served as a liaison between lead marketers, a sales force of over 1,500 agents, and all home office departments. Reduced costs and improved customer service through process improvements to internal systems.
- Created and implemented a product promotion financing system with an annual value of $675,000.
- Led a project team that analyzed and revised a management/agent/product information system. This 8-month project resulted in the production of a reliable field management reporting system.
- Analyzed and streamlined the new business and underwriting workflow process that reduced turnaround time by
  30 percent.

Supervisor, Commission Accounting, 1993–1994

- Ensured timely and accurate payment of commissions to 200 agents weekly and 5,000 agents monthly.
- Resolved issues through communication and teamwork with other departments.
- Trained and supervised a staff of three.

- Created and implemented a system that generated and monitored financial loans to agents.

Management Trainee/Internal Auditor, 1991–1993

- Performed departmental rotations through all administrative and sales support areas.
- Recovered more than $100,000 in erroneously paid agent commissions through monthly audits.

EDUCATION AND PROFESSIONAL AFFILIATIONS

Blue Wave University, Festus, MO
Master of Business Administration
(Management & Finance): 1999
Member of Beta Gamma Sigma Honor Society: 1999

University of Alabama, Tuscaloosa, AL.
Bachelor of Arts in Economics: 1991
Alabama Economic Society: 1991

Senior-Level Resume Example

WILLIAM JONES JOHNSON III

---

34 EASY STREET, NAPERVILLE, ILLINOIS 99999

555-505-1000 WJOHNSON@YOURISP.EDU

SUMMARY

Senior information technology executive, with a strong background in insurance, financial services, and technology. Significant experience in organizational transformation, systems management, reengineering, application development and delivery, team building, and expense management.

PROFESSIONAL EXPERIENCE

XYZ INSURANCE COMPANY, Maplegrove, MS, 1984–Present

The nation's largest publicly held personal lines insurer, XYZ provides insurance products to more than 14 million households and has approximately 13,000 exclusive agents in the U.S. and Canada.

Assistant Vice President, Marketing and Data Services, 2000–Present

- Managed a $74 million IT organization responsible for developing and supporting XYZ's corporate marketing processes including Customer Relationship (CRM), Data Warehousing, Document Management, Internet and Office Technologies, Customer Documents, and Billing.

- Created and led the Systems organization that supports the corporate and personal lines marketing processes, which resulted in the early delivery of several major CRM infrastructure components including campaign management, data mart, and desktop tools, a predictive modeling environment, and message brokering capabilities.

- Managed IT expenses to support marketing functions, resulting in a favorable 2001 year-end expense variance of $1.5 million (or 2 percent) on a budget of $74.2 million.

Assistant Vice President, Enterprise Technologies, 1998–2000

- Managed a $76 million Systems organization responsible for supporting XYZ's corporate financial, statistical, human resources, and professional office processes.

- Managed the IT expenses for the support of the back office and administrative functions, while continuing to upgrade XYZ's overall technology infrastructure. Delivered a favorable variance of $4.4 million (or 4.9 percent) on a 1999 budget of $89.5 million as well as a favorable variance of $4.7 million (or 6.1 percent) on a budget of $76.8 million in 2000.

- Created, funded, and directed a high-performance team that developed and implemented a client household database that enabled XYZ to interact seamlessly with customers via the Internet, a call center, or an agent.

- Created a high-performance team that developed a Comparative Rater application to analyze the competitive automobile pricing environment within five target market states. Pilot was delivered in 120 days and within budget.

Assistant Vice President, Application Architecture and Strategies, 1984–1998

- Managed a highly technical organization that established and maintained XYZ's systems architecture, architecture that set the company's strategic technology direction.
- Created, funded, and directed a Document Management initiative that developed and implemented a robust document archive and image infrastructure which resulted in fewer redundancies and overall cost reductions of several million dollars.
- Created, funded, and led a $20+ million Enterprise Data Warehousing initiative that developed and implemented a series of disciplined data management processes and a robust data warehousing infrastructure resulting in overall cost reductions of several million dollars. Created, funded, and directed a new communication team, resulting in more effective management of internal technology communications and external media releases.

Assistant Vice President, Reinvention Team, 1990–1995

- Participated on a senior-level business reengineering team commissioned by the chairman, CEO, and senior management.

- Created and led an Enterprise Architect team that established and maintained technology standards, resulting in a more highly disciplined IT development process with more effective use of technology resources.

- Created and led the development of the first enterprise Information Technology Strategic Plan, which provided a detailed roadmap for the major IT initiatives that would be required to support the anticipated growth of the company into the new millennium. Plan resulted in a highly disciplined, multiyear investment of more than $1 billion with fewer redundancies and lower overall infrastructure costs.

- Provided technology and organizational design consultation to the senior management team that successfully reengineered several major customer relationship processes, resulting in improved customer satisfaction and product development cycle time and lower overall expenses.

VANDALAY INSURANCE
Manager, Commercial Insurance Systems, 1978-1984

- Managed a $35 million Systems organization and data center, which supported the commercial insurance applications for three profit centers.

- Led the successful transformation of an internally focused Systems department into a client-focused I/T Consulting organization that was instrumental in the overall turnaround of the Commercial Insurance Division, resulting in reduced I/T expenses, increased productivity, and a dramatic improvement in client satisfaction.

- Created and led a senior management governance team and resource allocation process for prioritizing and funding major IT initiatives, resulting in an overall reduction in expenses and more effective allocation of technology resources.

EDUCATION

Northsouthern University, Columbia, TN
    Master of Business Administration, Accounting and Information Systems,1984
Red Clover University, Boulder Junction, WI
    Bachelor of Arts, Economics and Sociology,1978

PROFESSIONAL AFFILIATIONS

Colleges and Universities,1996–Present
    Officer sponsor of XYZ's Northsouthern University recruiting team

Society for Information Management (SIM) 1996–Present
    Member of Naperville Chapter
    Member of SIM International Executive Board—VP of Enterprise Programs

Life Office Management Association (LOMA) 1998–2001
    XYZ's representative to Property and Casualty Systems Committee

How Hard Are You Knocking?

Insurance Accounting and Systems Association (IASA) 1985–1990
Member, chaired systems research and program committees

National Association of Independent Insurers (NAII) 1985–1990
Member, Chaired Program Committee.

Cover Letter Examples

JANE DOE ADEAR
555 East Third Street
Jacksonville, Florida 22222
(555) 567-0000 <u>doeadear@isp.com</u>

April 17, 2010

Mr. John Smith
Director, Florida State Social Services
600 Water Street
Jacksonville, Florida 22222

Dear Mr. Smith:

In June 2010, I will receive my Bachelor of Arts degree from Florida State University, pending the completion of my foreign language requirement. I am writing to express my interest in obtaining a position with your agency. William Jones Johnson III recommended that I contact you.

As you will see from the enclosed resume, I majored in psychology and criminal justice, and achieved a 3.0 and 3.2 GPA, respectively. For the past one and a half years, I have been employed as a case manager for the Florida Temporary Homeless Shelter, and volunteered at the same agency for six months prior to my present employment. This experience has afforded me the opportunity to learn the functions of a homeless shelter and allowed me to participate in decisions regarding updating shelter policies and documentation procedures.

Realizing that this summary, as well as my resume, cannot adequately communicate my qualifications in depth, I would appreciate the opportunity to discuss with you in person how I might become an asset to your agency and will connect with you next week to set up an appointment.

Sincerely,

Jane Doe

Encl.

Emily B. A. Manager

430 Main Street

Pleasanton, California 65588

555-255-4227 MBA@yourISP.edu

September 1, 2009

Ms. Margaret Evans

Regional Director of Human Resources

Capital Corporation

Naperville, Illinois 33333

Dear Ms. Evans:

I am writing in reference to the vice president position that our mutual acquaintance, Amy Sell, recommended to me at the Capital Corporation.

My solid background in Fortune 100 telecommunications consulting and insurance marketing, product development, and operations has prepared me for the challenges confronting Capital in this economic downturn. I am confident that I can quickly help Capital capitalize on its assets in an era of economic turmoil.

I will call you next week to arrange a mutually convenient time to discuss how my expertise and experience can benefit Capital.

Best regards,

Emily B. A. Manager

Encl.

JAMES JACKSON
123 Wilson Drive

Phoenix, Arizona 11111

(555) 222-9999

September 5, 2009

Mr. Edward Smiles

Kodak Corporation

Rochester, New York 88888

Dear Mr. Smiles:

I am very interested in obtaining a position with Kodak Corporation where I can apply my educational background in technology to the field of telecommunications.

While attending the University of Colorado, I gained hands-on training for the latest technological advancements in the telecommunications field. In addition, as president of the American Marketing Association at UC, I designed new marketing efforts, which effectively increased membership over thirty percent in just one year. Further, as a student senator, I played an active part in crafting vision and mission statements for the student body.

I believe I would make an immediate and positive contribution to the Kodak Corporation. In addition, I am interested in the prospect of relocation to the upstate New York area. I would welcome an opportunity to discuss the possibility of employment with your firm. I will contact you next week to schedule a mutually convenient time to talk.

Sincerely,

James Jackson

Encl.

While your marketing campaign begins with your resume, it certainly doesn't end there. We have covered the nuts and bolts of resumes, cover letters and reference pages, which are key tools in your self-promotion campaign. They will help you sell yourself if you put the necessary time into making them perfect. If writing isn't your strong suit, seek help from your friends that do marketing for a living. You don't want your resume to be the reason you are rejected for a job. You want your resume to open the door to the next step in the process: the interview.

Chapter Checklist

✓ I have created a master resume that serves as the foundation of every resume I write.

✓ I have composed a generic cover letter that serves as a foundation of every cover letter I write.

✓ I understand how to write a cover letter that connects the dots from the job description to my resume.

✓ I have contacted six to eight references.

✓ I have a list of four to six references.

✓ I know how to articulate my skills and market value for various positions.

CHAPTER 8

HOW DO YOU LOOK?

Not sure how to dress for an interview? Read this chapter to learn what to wear and what not to wear. Remember: you only have one chance to make a good first impression. Therefore, your dress and visual presence can have a profound effect on your chances of obtaining the position you desire. Perception is everything. How the company views you, how you view yourself, and how you want others to view you all play a role in the "game" of interviewing. The manner in which you conduct yourself is just as important as what you say.

Insider's Tip: Did you know that about 85 percent of what you convey during this first impression is through nonverbal communication?

BASIC RULES

• *Dress appropriately for the industry*

Conservative firms—such as the financial, insurance, and accounting industries—require a very professional appearance. However, a relaxed or creative industry—marketing, advertising, and journalism—may be more impressed with a little more individualistic style. Regardless of the situation, flamboyance is not a wise choice! You want to be remembered for what you say, what you have done, and what you can offer to the company.

• *Dress in a manner that conforms to the specific company*

Take a look around the office during your informational interview, or even pop in the building some day before your real interview to get a sense of the culture and dress norms. Look at how the employees are dressed. You should strive to dress equally with the managers who might be conducting the interview. When in doubt, dress up, not down. It is always better to be more professionally dressed rather than less. While many firms today allow casual dress on a daily basis, you should be professionally dressed unless instructed to dress casually by the recruiter.

Personal hygiene is a necessity. Be sure your hair is neat and clean. Make sure your fingernails are clean and trimmed. Check for stains or wrinkles in your clothing. Avoid excessive cologne. Take a look into the mirror before you leave for the interview to conduct one last check of your appearance. Finally, make sure you brush your teeth or take breath mints with you!

Avoid distractions. Preferably, avoid wearing anything that identifies any beliefs or personal associations, such as religious jewelry or political buttons. In addition, avoid wearing any items that are considered masculine for a woman or feminine for a man (for example, a necktie for a woman or an earring on a man). These items are often distractions and could take the interviewer's attention away from what you have to say.

FOR WOMEN

When choosing the clothing for an interview, **the fit of your clothing** is the most important thing to consider. Uncomfortable clothing will make an already uncomfortable situation worse. You have more important things to worry about than your suit being too small, shoes being too tight, or blouse sleeves being too short. If you plan to shop for an interview suit, be sure to do it a couple of weeks ahead of time. Then you don't have to select an outfit at the last minute. Shopping early also gives you the opportunity to shop for matching accessories.

The best attire for corporate interviews is a **suit**. A basic blazer and matching skirt are preferred. Slacks are also considered professional attire for the interview stage. A dress may be worn, but is not recommended for the first interview. If a dress is worn, it should be a professional-looking dress, preferably with a blazer.

When wearing a suit, the blazer should be fairly conservative. Extra-wide collars or other trendy designs have no positive impact in an interview. A double-breasted suit tends to look more professional, whereas the single is more casual; either is acceptable.

Avoid big bright buttons or other distracting items attached to the blazer; these only divert the interviewer's attention. The skirt should be right around knee length, or perhaps one to two inches above. Shorter lengths are not recommended.

The type of **material** can make or break the suit. Wool is the preferred material, but consider the climate and season. A lighter weight material such as linen or quality blends may be sufficient. We stress the word "quality." You should wear clothing that looks as if it is of high quality.

As for **color**, when in doubt, wear navy blue. Although other colors may suffice, navy blue is still considered classic. Again, depending on the perception you want to instill and the type of company you are interviewing with, other colors may be worn. Shades of gray are also considered conservative. Certainly, some sort of dark-colored suit is preferred for the first interview and black is a safe choice as well.

The **second interview** may allow for more freedom in color choice, such as dark green, red, or brown. During the second interview, you may also wear a classic dress with a jacket. A small print in the fabric is also acceptable as long as it does not divert the attention of the interviewer. Pastels are generally not good interviewing suit colors.

Your suit should be neat, pressed, and free of lint, which displays to the interviewer a pride in appearance. The time you took to prepare for the interview is taken into consideration. If your suit is wrinkled, you appear as if you did not plan ahead for the interview and do not care about getting the job.

Generally, a **blouse or shell** should be worn underneath the blazer. Absolutely never wear camisoles. They do not convey the right impression in an interview. The blouse should not be transparent and should not be cut too low in the front. The blouse should be crisp and clean. A white blouse does a good job of giving a bright, clean look. Cream and ivory are also acceptable colors. Finally, the blouse should not be too frilly or have too large of a bow or other designs, as these cause distractions.

Proper **accessories** can help make a great first impression. Choose hosiery to match the bottom of your skirt. For instance, if the bottom of the skirt is black, wear black nylons; if navy, wear navy ones. If matching the skirt is not possible, wear nude nylons or skin matching nylons. The idea is to create one solid flow from head to toe with no distractions. If you have a white blouse, black skirt, and white nylons, there is a distraction in the flow. When in doubt, go for the nude-colored nylons.

Shoes are an equally important part of the attire. Many people do not realize that shoes are very noticeable items, especially if they do not conform to the rest of the outfit. Make sure they look professional and are shined. They should be sensible and not too flashy. Try to avoid decorative designs or fancy bows. They should be slip on, rather than with some sort of tying or buckling required. Proper fit should also be considered as you may be wearing them for a long time. Pumps are good interviewing shoes for women. A small to medium half inch to two-inch heel is suggested for all women, regardless of height. Your shoes should also match the bottom of your skirt, which continues the visual flow without distractions.

A small amount of **jewelry** may enhance your appearance. However, the idea is to keep it simple. The best bet would be to wear just earrings and a watch. A nice dress watch is certainly acceptable and can come in handy to avoid being late. Avoid plastic, large-faced watches. A simple gold, silver, or even conservative leather-strapped watch is appropriate. Earrings are great accessories that seem to set off the face in a positive way. The best ones are small to medium in size and cover the lower one-quarter to one-third part of the earlobe. It is preferable to wear either gold or silver. Wear only one earring per ear; do not wear dangling earrings. Other jewelry may be worn, but should be kept to a minimum. Rings are acceptable, but try to limit them to one or two per hand. Conservative bracelets are acceptable, but should be kept to a minimum and should not include bangle bracelets (they tend to clank and make noise).

A necklace may be worn as well. However, only wear one necklace and avoid large pendants. Small to medium-sized pins on a lapel are attractive and professional, but remember to stay simple. The best rule of thumb is to prevent distracting attention with your jewelry. Remember, you want the interviewer to remember you, not the earrings or bracelets you wore.

Finally, men and women should be careful when applying **fragrances**. It is actually a better idea to go without cologne for an interview. An allergic reaction by the interviewer could cause the interview to end quickly. If you must wear cologne, better to apply just a small bit rather than to overdo it.

The following chart summarizes the dos and don'ts of dressing the part for women.

Women

Wear	*Avoid*
Suit - navy, gray, dark green, black, burgundy, dark brown	purple, yellow, pastels
Blouse - Silk-like fabric feminine/subtle design white, cream, ivory pastels	low-cut shirts
Skirt - 1–2" above the knee conservative slit up back or side	higher than 2" above knee 1" below calf muscle high slits
Shoes - Pumps	high heels (above 2") stilettos
0–2" heel	uncomfortable fit/new shoes
Accessories - One earring per ear two rings maximum dress watch lapel pin nude or tan nylons	bangle bracelets several necklaces piercing (other than ear) political or religious pins white or any other color nylons

FOR MEN

The basic interview attire for a man is a **suit**. Again, look to the industry and individual company to gain a perspective of how to dress. For a conservative company or industry, a single-breasted suit is recommended. A single-breasted suit is one in which the buttons and the jacket opening are vertical. With a double-breasted suit, the jacket that has overlapping fronts that gives a double thickness of cloth. For a less conservative firm, we recommend a double-breasted suit. When in doubt, dress more conservatively and wear a single-breasted suit.

When selecting a suit, consider your body type. Short or stocky body types should avoid the double-breasted suit, which makes you appear heavier than you are. Ask for the help of experienced sales personnel in the men's department of your local department store or a men's shop where suits are sold. They often have the best advice for fitting your body type.

The suit **material** should be wool. High-quality blended suits are also acceptable but often do not last as long and do not lie on one's body correctly after repeated cleanings. Quality is key. You should put as much emphasis on your suit as your resume. A high-quality suit shows attention to detail and pride in appearance.

The **color** of the suit should be conservative, usually navy or shades of gray. Stay away from pinstripe suits. These suits have traditionally been power suits and are usually worn by executives. You may appear to be a threat or perceived as a corporate climber if your clothing is too flashy.

Your **necktie** should also be a conservative color. You want to offset the color of the suit, but you don't want to take the interviewer's attention away from you. With a navy blue suit, you could wear a blue or red tie with some type of design. Try to stay away from pastels or flashy loud designs. Usually the salesperson where you purchase your suit and tie knows what you are looking for and can recommend and match accordingly. Use your best judgment, and consult your friends about what looks good and what does not. Avoid being trendy but don't look dowdy either!

Your **shirt** is also an important part of the interviewing outfit. Again, it depends on the color of the suit. A white, 100 percent cotton shirt cleaned and pressed with light starch is always a good idea. Quality cotton/polyester shirts are also good, keeping quality in mind. You want to show the interviewer that you focus on quality in everything you do. With a single-breasted suit, a pointed collar shirt looks more professional. With a double-breasted suit, the button-down collar is more professional. Above all else, make sure the shirt fits well and allows room for flexibility.

The best **shoes** to wear for an interview are wingtips or nice loafers. Do not wear trendy loafers, boots, or boat shoes, as these present a more trendy or casual look. The color of the shoes depends on your suit. The most common colors worn by professionals have been cordovan or black shoes.

Along with your shoes, **socks** are very important. Make sure they match your suit and are of high quality. Make sure your socks cover your calf muscle. You do not want to expose any leg skin when you cross your legs. Do not wear socks with holes in the toes or heels. What would happen if the interviewer asked you to take your shoes off to walk in his or her office? (Don't worry, this doesn't happen often, but it is best to be prepared.)

You also want your **belt** to be in good condition without signs of wear. Make sure you did not miss any belt loops. If the interviewer asks you to remove your jacket, your belt will show.

The following chart summarizes the dos and don'ts of dressing the part for men.

MEN

Wear	_Avoid_
Suit - navy, back, shades of gray 100 percent wool quality blends	brown, pinstripe poor polyester blend
Shoes - wingtips professional loafers, tasseled shoes	Crocs, sandals, boat shoes
Shirt - white, light blue small stripe, pastels pressed and clean	large stripes dark colors

Tie - blue, red, designs	yellow, crazy/funny
subtle print	loud stripes
Accessories - one ring at most	earrings, bracelets
belt matches shoes	tie clips or collar bars
dress watch	handkerchief in pocket

FOR MEN AND WOMEN

Don't forget that the most important thing to wear is a smile. Keep a positive mental attitude. An invitation to interview is an accomplishment. Be enthusiastic. Stand tall, but not stiffly. Show the interviewer you are ready and willing to help this company succeed and hit the ground running.

In addition, remember a few other tips. Take a **lint roller** with you to take off any dog hair, lint, or dandruff.

Make sure you take a **damp washcloth** in your car, which you can use to clean and shine your shoes one last time, giving the interviewer the impression of well-groomed shoes.

Finally, do not forget to take items that are needed for elements such as snow and rain. Take an **umbrella** if it is raining. This little detail makes a big difference for an interview. If it is snowing, feel free to wear **boots** to the interview and carry your dress shoes. Change in the lobby if needed. The last thing you want to think about during the interview is wet socks and pants because you had to walk through the snow.

We understand that this discussion sounds very basic, but people often forget the smallest details.

Before you leave your house, make sure you cover all the basics. Your **hair** should be well groomed. We recommend using hair spray to keep it in place. If you have a trendy hairstyle, you might consider toning it down for the interview to match your conservative professional appearance.

When you look in the mirror, you must feel good about your appearance and not focus on it. During the interview you should be focused on what you want to say. Give the interviewer your best for his or her first impression. Take care of yourself and your appearance. Good luck and look your best!

Chapter Checklist

✓ I have a neatly pressed interview suit in my closet ready for the next call to interview.

✓ I have an emergency clothing tool kit (lint brush, washcloth, shoe shiner, umbrella) ready to hit the road for my next interview.

✓ I keep aware of clothing trends (or have a trusted friend who does) and update my wardrobe every year.

CHAPTER 9

THE INTERVIEW

Preparation is essential for an interview. Don't be blindsided during an interview. Prepare answers to every question that may be asked of you. Be ready to close the deal. Learn strategies to succeed in any interview situation.

Receiving an invitation to interview is a sign that you are conducting a successful job search. You passed the resume test and likely found a position that is a good professional fit for you. This chapter will explore the different types of interviews you might face, the topics that are most likely to be covered in the interview, and techniques to prepare before the interview. We will cover what to expect after the first interview and how to deal with rejection, acceptance, and salary negotiation.

Be prepared! Through this process, you will need to deliver the thirty-second commercial described in an earlier chapter on networking. This professional pitch comes in handy when preparing to articulate your strengths in an interview situation.

"TELL ME ABOUT YOURSELF"

The first task of successful interviewing is answering the ubiquitous and difficult, "Tell me about yourself" prompt. This is a simple request with a complicated answer. Whether you are meeting a stranger in the elevator, responding to an interviewer's prompt, or shaking hands at a networking event, you need to know how to respond. If you are prepared to answer this question, you will be prepared for unexpected opportunities.

Don't ever respond by giving your life story, bragging, or wasting time talking about some trite interest. The request begs an answer that continues the conversation in a compelling manner. Convince the other person that you are interested and bring value to any enterprise. The most powerful response will articulate your strengths and competitive advantages over the next candidate. This is not the time to be humble, shy, or embarrassed.

Be strong, strategic, and succinct. **Know your selling points**. Describe the kind of problems that you solve better than anyone else does. Figure out what is truly unique and valuable about you and lay it on the table.

Whether you can conjugate verbs in Swahili, sell tricycles to seniors, or create mosaic masterpieces, be ready to **share a short story** about how this skill brings value to others. If you honestly don't know your strengths, complete career assessments, work with a career counselor, review your performance evaluations or simply watch a colleague and assess what you can do better, quicker, or more creatively.

Finally, remember to **think micro and macro**. After you take a microscope to yourself, use binoculars to figure out the path ahead. Know who you are so you can determine where you are going. Think about how you can most effectively interact with the world in a way that brings true personal satisfaction.

Insider's Tip: Keep in mind that the interview is not an interrogation. It is a two-way conversation. Be curious, engaged, and ready with questions. Don't be intimidated; you are interviewing them as much as they are interviewing you. Remember, they once were in your shoes, and they put their pants on one leg at a time just like you. In fact, many employers find interviewing very stressful.

THE FOUR TYPES OF INTERVIEWS

You need to understand the different types of interviews you may face during your job search. The four most common types of interviews are:

1. Phone interview

2. Face-to-face interview

3. Group interview

4. Meal interview

Phone Interview

The phone interview is the most common interview and is usually the first step in the interview process. The objective of a phone interview is for the recruiter or hiring manager to learn a little more about your background in order to properly screen out the candidates who do not match the position description. Position descriptions are generally internal documents that highlight the skills that are needed for an open position. The interviewer will use these documents to determine whether a candidate has the appropriate qualifications for a given position.

Here are a few tips we recommend for phone interviews.

- When the phone interview is scheduled, ask the interviewer if you can be the one to initiate the call. For example, if the interviewer calls you and schedules the interview for 3 p.m. Tuesday, ask if you can call them. Doing so reduces your stress level prior to the interview and gives you a psychological edge. You are ready for the interview as soon as you begin dialing the phone. If you wait for them to call you, you will be stressed fifteen minutes prior to the call waiting for them to call you. However, if the interview is scheduled for 3 p.m., you need to call at 3 p.m. on the dot.
- Dress professionally for the phone interview. When you are dressed professionally, you feel and act much more professional. Consider this a formal interview.

- Prepare the house or apartment for the interview. Let everyone know that you will be on the phone for an interview.

- Sit at a table where you can utilize your notes or stand near your notes. Standing can help project your voice, which illustrates confidence. The phone interview is like an open book test. Assemble your materials: resume, job description, company's annual report, or company marketing materials. Just make sure you don't make noise with your notes or with your computer!

- Be familiar with this information already. Read the annual report BEFORE the interview.

- Never conduct a phone interview on a cell phone as you may lose the connection during the call.

- Disable call waiting. If you forget, never click over to answer a call on call waiting. It is perceived as rude.

- Make sure you ask at least three to five questions about the company at the end of the interview. If you did your research prior to the interview, you can ask questions about your findings—for example, "I noticed during my research that XYZ Company is planning to grow by ten percent next year. Where do you feel that growth will come from?"

- At the end of the phone interview, make sure you close with a few questions about your interaction with the company. "Did I answer your questions to your satisfaction? Do my qualifications match your position criteria?"

If they answer yes, ask about next steps and expectations of the face-to-face interview. If the interviewer answers no, meaning you did not match the position criteria, ask for constructive criticism and listen. Do not defend yourself. Use the information you gather for improving your next interview. Remember to thank the interviewer for his or her time and conclude the call pleasantly.

A typical phone interview lasts approximately twenty to forty minutes. The topics most likely to be covered are your background and experience, your education, your job desires (what type of job you want), your salary expectations, your strengths as they apply to the job, and your perception of your weaknesses. A sample of an interviewer's phone interview script appears below.

Sample Telephone Interview Script

Candidate name_____   Date_____

Where did you hear about the position/company?

_____

Current company_____   Dates_____

Why are you looking for a new job? (Reasons for leaving previous positions/employment gaps)

Current Compensation:

      Base:

      Bonus:

      Benefits:

      Desired:

What type of position are you interested in?

Commuting/travel issues (if applicable):

      Education:

      School:

      Degree:

      Certifications:

      Desire to continue:

What is your current availability?

How Hard Are You Knocking?

Are you interviewing anywhere else?

>Status:

>Desire:

What are the most important factors in accepting a new job?

Work experience:

>Software languages, if applicable

>Lead role (leadership)

>Level of contacts (sales)

>Size of accounts (sales)

>Amount sold in revenue (sales)

>Quality testing methods (QA)

>Sales methods (sales)

>Work environment (team)

Face-to-Face Interview

When you pass the phone interview, you'll be called in for a face-to-face interview. This interview takes place with the hiring manager for the position (your future boss) or by a human resource staff member, or both. Whoever it is, make sure you follow the interview guidelines to help you prepare. Wear a formal suit for all interviews. While some companies dress in business casual for daily business, we recommend wearing a suit for the first interview to make a positive first impression. When arriving for the interview, be sure to show up fifteen minutes ahead of the scheduled time, which gives you time to mentally prepare, locate the office, study the corporate materials in the lobby and to have one last look at yourself in the restroom before the interview.

Remember to be personable with the receptionist. In some companies, the receptionist is an important part of the interview process. The company may want to find out how you treat others in the company and how you make a first impression. We recommend introducing yourself and explaining that you were scheduled for an interview with Mr. or Ms. _____ at 3 p.m. The receptionist may be a good source of company information. You may want to ask him or her questions about the company if you have time and the receptionist appears receptive. Look around the lobby and notice the interaction between employees. Read company literature if it is available while you are waiting.

What to bring to an interview

You need to prepare a few items ahead of time and bring them to the interview in a professional portfolio.

149

You should have **three printed copies of your resume** on professional resume paper. Do not bring photocopied resumes. You should also consider bringing an electronic copy of your resume on a flash drive. This way you can be certain that the interviewer or hiring manager has an electronic copy of your resume to share with others.

Have a list of possible **references** on a separate piece of paper. We recommend listing a previous boss, a professor from your school (if you are a recent graduate), and a professional peer as possible references. Use the resume paper for these references which will list your references name, title, address, phone number, email address as well as your relationship with the reference. However, before you list your references, make sure you obtain their permission.

You should be prepared to complete a **job application**. Bring the pertinent information with you when you arrive at the interview, which will help you complete an application. You should have information about your previous employment, including the dates worked, address and phone number, previous manager's name, and salary information. Bring these documents with you so that the application details are not something you are struggling to remember. You will have many things on your mind to consider, and the last thing you should have to worry about is completing an application.

A sample application is included here for your review. Fill in every blank for optimal results, and bring a completed copy with you on interviews.

Sample Application for Employment

PLEASE PRINT

Equal access to programs, services, and employment is available to all persons.

Those applicants requiring reasonable accommodation to the application and/or interview process should notify a representative of the Human Resources Department.

Position(s) applied for _____ Date of application

_____

Name _____ Social Security #

_____

(Last Name, First Name & Middle Name)

Address _____

(Street, City, State, Zip Code)

Telephone #_____ Mobile/Beeper/Other Phone #

_____

Email Address _____

If you are under 18, and it is required, can you furnish a work permit?
Yes   No
If no, please explain _____

Have you ever been employed here before? Yes   No
If yes, give dates and positions _____

How Hard Are You Knocking?

Are you legally eligible for employment in this country? Yes   No

Date available for work_____ What is your desired salary range?

_____

Type of employment desired:

Full-Time Part-Time Temporary Seasonal Educational Co-Op

Are you able to meet the attendance requirements of the position? Yes
No

Have you ever pled "guilty" or "no contest" to or been convicted of a
crime? Yes   No

If yes, please provide date(s) and details_____

ANSWERING "YES" TO THESE QUESTIONS DOES NOT CON-
STITUTE AN AUTOMATIC BAR TO EMPLOYMENT. FACTORS
SUCH AS DATE OF THE OFFENSE, SERIOUSNESS AND NA-
TURE OF THE VIOLATION, REHABILITATION, AND POSI-
TION APPLIED FOR WILL BE TAKEN INTO ACCOUNT.

Driver's license number if driving is an essential job function _____
State _____

Employment History

Provide the following information of your past three (3) employers,
assignments, or volunteer activities, starting with the most recent.

1.

From   To   Employer Telephone #

Starting Job Title/ Address

Final Job Title

Summarize the Nature of Work Performed and Supervisor and Title

Job Responsibilities

May We Contact for Reference?   Yes No Later

Reason for Leaving Hourly Rate/Salary

Start $_____   Per_____   Final $_____   Per_____

2.

From   To   Employer Telephone #

Starting Job Title/ Address

Final Job Title

Summarize the Nature of Work Performed and Supervisor and Title

Job Responsibilities

May We Contact for Reference?   Yes No Later

Reason for Leaving Hourly Rate/Salary

Start $_____   Per_____   Final $_____   Per_____

3.

From   To   Employer Telephone #

Starting Job Title/ Address

Final Job Title

Summarize the Nature of Work Performed and Supervisor and Title

Job Responsibilities

How Hard Are You Knocking?

May We Contact for Reference?   Yes No Later

Reason for Leaving Hourly Rate/Salary

Start $_____   Per_____   Final $_____   Per_____

AN EQUAL OPPORTUNITY EMPLOYER

Skills and Qualifications

Summarize any training, skills, licenses, and/or certificates that may qualify you as being able to perform job-related functions in the position for which you are applying.

Educational Background (if job related)

Name and Number of Years

Did You Graduate?   Course of Study

Location Completed

High School

College Major

Degree

Other

References

Name_____ Telephone _____ Number of Years Known _____

Name_____ Telephone _____ Number of Years Known _____

Name_____ Telephone _____ Number of Years Known _____

Applicant Statement

I certify that all information I have provided in order to apply for and secure work with the employer is true, complete, and correct. I understand that any information provided by me that is found to be false, incomplete, or misrepresented in any respect will be sufficient cause to

(i) cancel further consideration of this application or (ii) immediately discharge me from the employer's service, whenever it is discovered.

I expressly authorize, without reservation, the employer, its representatives, employees, or agents to contact and obtain information from all references (personal and professional), employers, public agencies, licensing authorities and educational institutions and to otherwise verify the accuracy of all information provided by me in this application, resume, or job interview.

I hereby waive any and all rights and claims I may have regarding the employer, its agents, employees, or representatives, for seeking, gathering, and using such information in the employment process and all other persons, corporations, or organizations for furnishing such information about me.

I understand that the employer does not unlawfully discriminate in employment and no question on this application is used for the purpose of limiting or excusing any applicant from consideration for employment on a basis prohibited by applicable local, state, or federal law.

I understand that this application remains current for only 30 days. At the conclusion of that time, if I have not heard from the employer and still wish to be considered for employment, it will be necessary to reapply and fill out a new application.

If I am hired, I understand that I am free to resign at any time, with or without cause and without prior notice, and the employer reserves the same right to terminate my employment at any time, with or without cause and without prior notice, except as may be required by law.

This application does not constitute an agreement or contract for employment for any specified period or definite duration. I understand that no supervisor or representative of the employer is authorized to make any assurances to the contrary and that no implied, oral, or written agreements contrary to the foregoing express language are valid unless they are in writing and signed by the employer's president. I also understand that if I am hired, I will be required to provide proof of identity and legal authority to work in the United States and that federal immigration laws require me to complete an I-9 Form in this regard.

DO NOT SIGN UNTIL YOU HAVE READ THE ABOVE APPLICANT STATEMENT.

I certify that I have read, fully understand, and accept all terms of the foregoing Applicant Statement.

Signature of Applicant _____   Date _____ /_____ /_____

Your signature gives the employer the ability to complete a background check. Typically, the background check verifies past employment including dates, positions and compensation. The background check also checks state and federal criminal records (typically felonies), and educational background including school, major and degrees. You should be prepared to share this type of information when you arrive for the interview.

Once you arrive at your interview, remember to make a positive first impression. You should make sure you look and feel like you can take on the world. Make sure you follow the guidelines in the "Dressing for Business" chapter of this book. The face-to-face interview is an opportunity for you to sell yourself in person. Take your time and think about every answer.

The period for a face-to-face interview is typically one hour. However, in some cases, they may ask that you interview with different people from the company. We recommend that you have five to ten questions typed and prepared to ask during the interviews.

Make sure your questions show that you did your homework, such as: "I noticed in your annual report that you were planning to expand into Europe. What is driving that decision?" You may also take notes during the interview, but be sure to ask the interviewer for permission before you start taking notes. Finally, the interview is just a meeting between two people. They are evaluating you on your personality, cultural fit, experience, education, skills, and knowledge. Just be yourself.

Group Interview

The third type of interview is a group interview. Often, it is done because it is time effective and allows a number of staff members to evaluate a candidate. The group interview is much like the face-to-face interview except that you have multiple people interviewing you, and even the seating arrangement can be intimidating. Instead of sitting in an office at a small table or desk, you may be front and center at the head of a conference table.

Group interviews are common with very stressful jobs such as a social worker or police officer. The group interview evaluates how you deal with the stress of a group setting and how you deal with multiple questions. The best guideline is for you to stay calm and answer each question much like a face-to-face interview. Take your time and speak to each person in the room. Ask each interviewer a question at the end of the interview to show that you are engaged and interested. This time also presents an opportunity for you to evaluate the personality of the company by talking with each person and watching their interaction and nonverbal behavior.

Don't forget to write **personalized thank-you notes** to each member of the interview committee. In your note, try to comment specifically on a question that he or she asked or had concerns about.

Group interviews with multiple candidates at a networking event are also common. Many companies prefer this approach and use it routinely. It is important in these situations, that you monitor your non-verbal behavior and display the utmost courtesy to the other candidates. Don't think for one moment that you can relax; you must keep your interview game face on the whole time!

The most important guideline is to take your time and think through each question and answer, which will be a bit more stressful than a one-on-one interview. Your preparation is critical. In some cases, you can ask the recruiter, who is scheduling your interview, what type of interview you can expect. If you follow these guidelines, you will be very prepared for whatever type of interview you face.

Meal Interview

The final type of interview is the meal interview. The meal interview typically takes place during lunch hours and involves the hiring manager. Either the hiring manager is interviewing you during lunch because his/her schedule is too busy or because the manager wants to see how you interact in public, especially if you are interviewing for a customer-service position such as sales.

Whatever the reason, these guidelines can help you do well. The first guideline is to **make sure you eat before the interview**. This advice may be counterintuitive since the interview will be held during a meal, but because you will be doing most of the talking, the last thing you want to be doing is staring at the manager's sandwich with your mouth salivating because you are hungry. Of course, you will still order a meal. However, the meal will be to nibble on during the conversation.

The second rule is to **bring money or a credit card** with you just in case the manager does not pay. This scenario is unlikely, but it is always best to be prepared.

The third guideline is to **order something simple** and easy to eat. One of the main concerns that stress out job candidates on meal interviews is what to order. You do not want to eat something that is sloppy. In addition, you also don't want to order something outrageously expensive. My recommendation is for you to ask the interviewer what meal(s) they recommend. This question eliminates your worry about cost because they are recommending the dish. A safe bet is to order some sort of salad or chicken entrée.

Avoid ordering anything that needs to be eaten with your hands. Also keep in mind that you don't want to order a rare steak and then need to send it back to the kitchen. Never send food back to the kitchen during a meal interview.

The fourth guideline is to **never order alcohol.** Even if the interviewer orders a double shot of whiskey with a martini chaser, never follow suit. The interviewer's action could be a test to see if you would drink on the job. In addition, drinking impairs your responses, no matter what your tolerance. Just kindly say, "No thanks, I will have the lemonade."

Treat this meeting as formal as a face-to-face interview, but make sure you interact with the server as well as the host when you are being seated. Remember, the interviewer is also evaluating your behavior in public. Most importantly, make sure you have **good manners** when

161

you are having lunch. Do not eat with your mouth open or remove orthodontic appliances in public, for example.

Finally, take along your **portfolio** with your resume and questions inside, just like for the face-to-face interview. Don't relax for a moment. It's even more essential on a meal interview that you reflect professional polish and social ease.

INTERVIEW TOPICS

Now that we have explored the types of interviews you could face, let's review the type of topics that the interviews cover. As you prepare for the interviews and do your research on your target companies, make sure you think about your answers to the following topics.

Experience

One obviously important topic is your experience as it applies to the position for which you are interviewing. Make sure you fully understand the position's qualifications as stated in the job posting, on the employer's website, or through a position description you gathered during your research.

Be prepared for questions such as, "Why should I hire you for this position?" "What makes you more qualified than the other candidates that we are interviewing?" or "Relate your past experience to this position." Try to review your resume as well as the accomplishments list that you developed earlier in the book. Apply your accomplishments to these types of questions. The employer is looking to find a connection between your past experience and the opening he or she has to fill. They want to know that you can hit the ground running and solve on-the-job problems immediately.

Company knowledge

The second topic that might be covered is company knowledge. The interviewer's questions would probably include "Why do you want to work for XYZ Company?" or "Tell me about my company." Make sure you have researched the company thoroughly. These questions sound like a test, and guess what? They are a test. Do your homework and you won't fail the test! Mention the website, the annual report, and information you gathered during any informational interviews. Remember, many candidates are applying for this same job. You need to differentiate yourself by showing that you went the extra mile with your research on this company.

Communication skills

The third topic is your communication skills, which are evaluated during the interview. Our research shows the most important attribute a candidate can have is the ability to communicate. Interviewers might ask questions such as "Tell me about a time when you had to give bad news to a person" or "Tell me how you would sell my company to your friends." Remain confident. Confidence shows through and allows you to communicate in an effective manner. The interviewer is looking for confidence, knowledge, and proper grammar. Practice with family and friends.

Teamwork

The fourth topic is teamwork. The interviewer is evaluating your ability to function in a team environment. In today's business world, many companies are focusing on teams as part of their cultures. When you are preparing for the interview, think about when you were part of a team. What was the task? Who made up the team? How did the team interact? Who was the team leader? Most importantly, what was the outcome? If you are new to the workforce, these experiences can be related to high school sports, club activities, or group projects at school. The interviewer is looking for your attitude toward teamwork and your successes and failures in team settings. Think about your most memorable team experience and prepare your thoughts to respond to this topic during the interview.

Leadership experience

The fifth topic is your leadership experience. The interviewer is evaluating your potential as a leader and is using your past leadership examples as a gauge for the evaluation. This topic can also draw on your high school, club, or community service activities.

Try to remember when you were put in charge of a project, task, or team. How did you approach the task? Were you a motivational leader or a leader who earned the group's respect by doing? Did you delegate the activities and follow a project plan, or did you allow the team to choose the tasks to achieve the goal at hand? The interviewer looks for these types of things.

When you think about your experiences, write them down on a piece of paper. Try to choose the one experience that could apply to the position you are interviewing for and expand your thoughts on that experience.

This level of solid preparation, which your competition might not be considering, allows you to be more prepared for the interview, thus reducing your stress and increasing your chances of success.

Educational experience

Another important interview topic especially relevant for recent graduates is your educational experience. The interviewer is looking for information about your decision to attend your particular college or university, as well as why you chose your specific major and your knowledge within that major.

Prepare for questions about your favorite and least favorite classes as well as your favorite professor and reasons for all your answers. The reason we ask these types of questions in our interviews is to evaluate what motivates you. If we know that you liked a class because it was always new and exciting, we can feel more comfortable placing you in a job that challenges you and subjects you to frequent change. If we know that you are motivated by a teacher who pushes you to do better, we would want to place you in a position that has that style of manager or leader. Finally, knowing why you chose your major helps us evaluate your motivation. If we know that you are motivated by money, for example, we may want to put you in a sales job.

Your college major is important as a backdrop of knowledge. However, you should know that only thirty percent of students actually end up working in their major after college. The major is important because it gives you a foundation of knowledge. An employer will not necessarily hire you to be an accountant just because you majored in accounting and are a solid accountant. The employer will hire you because you can *scale up*. You have a baseline of knowledge upon which they can build. Most college students do not have work experience, which is okay. However, if you have a solid foundation, you have a much better chance to succeed.

Logic/Critical Thinking

A characteristic that interviewers are looking for is logical thinking. Take your time and think about each question. Do not try to answer with words you think the interviewer wants to hear. Think about the questions, and answer them to the best of your ability.

Remember, you have done a significant amount of preparation for the interview. Make sure you answer the exact questions they ask. Read their nonverbal signals and finish your answer. Remember, interviewers put their pants on one leg at a time just like the rest of us. They are people looking to hire a person who matches the requirements. If you prepare for the interview using these guidelines, you will excel and land the job you are looking for.

SAMPLE INTERVIEW QUESTIONS

Now that you are aware of some typical interview topics, consider some examples of questions that an interviewer may ask you. Each set of questions is contained within a general area of knowledge that the interviewer is evaluating. Below the questions, we have included the evaluation criteria that each set of questions uncovers about the candidate. (Note that while these questions apply to past jobs, they can also be answered relative to time in school or college.)

Collaboration and Teamwork

How have you gone about developing a cohesive, high-functioning team atmosphere in the past? How would you do it at my company?

In your last position, how would your previous coworkers describe you? What was it like to work with you? What would they say about your collaboration and teamwork style?

Give examples of how you have brought out the best in others in a team environment.

Tell me about a time when you had to deal with a difficult coworker. What made him/her difficult? What did you do? What was the outcome?

Tell me about a time when you were a leader and a follower?

How Hard Are You Knocking?

The right answers reveal your history of succeeding in a team environment, success working in teams, ability to handle team conflicts, and grace in making teammates look good.

Communication

What are your strengths with respect to communication skills? What aspects of communication would you like to further develop?

If we ask your last boss, how will he or she describe your writing skills? What are your strengths and developmental needs in this regard?

In what ways was written communication required in your previous jobs? What materials or samples of your writing best demonstrate your writing skills? Describe the technical documents you have written in your past two jobs.

How would your colleagues and/or boss describe your communication skills?

The right answers reveal your ability to write effectively with specific project examples, a history of strong communication skills, ability to speak clearly and intelligently and convey important concepts and ideas.

Influencing

In your current job, describe a situation where you were required to persuade or influence someone to your point of view. What was your approach? How did the other person respond? What happened?

How would you describe your style of persuasion? What are your strengths? In what ways do you need to become more effective? How do people typically respond to your style of persuasion?

Think of someone who comes to mind as being especially persuasive. Who? Why is this person persuasive? What have you learned from him or her? How has this person influenced your style?

Give an example of where you had to bring the best of your persuasion skills into play. What did you do? What skills did you use?

The right answers reveal your ability to sell ideas and gain buy in from others. Your resume shows your ability to establish rapport, appropriate persuasive style of conversation.

Achievement Focus

What would people who know you well say about your ability to overcome setbacks, adversity, or failure? Be specific and give some examples.

What has been your greatest personal success regarding your academic or professional career? Why do you consider this to be your greatest success?

Discuss your key accomplishments in your last two positions (professional or academic). How have you added value in key roles you've held?

In your last two jobs or internships, discuss your performance and how you met your goals.

Describe your performance in relation to these expectations and goals.

Describe some important setbacks or failures that you've experienced. What did you do in response to these situations?

If you were to create a list of career highlights, what would be on it? Why?

The right answers reveal a clear picture of achievement and drive to succeed and the ability to overcome adversity.

Initiative

What would people who know you well say about your level of initiative and the extent to which you know when action is a priority? Be specific and provide some examples.

Give me an indication of the extent to which you are comfortable making decisions on your own without input from your boss. Convince me you are able to make decisions and take action on your own.

Do you react better to a lot of direction or minimal direction from others?

What would your previous employer say about your ability to meet demands in a timely manner? Tell me about steps you've taken to ensure that required work is completed.

How would you rate your ability to remain persistent and follow through on work commitments? Give me some examples that support your assessment.

What would your previous boss say about your willingness to take responsibility for your work, and to what extent would he or she say you took ownership of your projects or commitments?

In your current or previous jobs, on what occasions did you feel you should consult with your boss before proceeding with some action? When did you feel it was proper to act on your own?

Describe a time during your past two positions or internships in which you went above and beyond what it took to get the job done. Describe the situation and what you did.

The right answers reveal your commitment to go above and beyond the call of duty, comfort with making decisions, discernment in asking for input, and a high level of ownership for your work.

Customer Focus

Describe your approach to directly impact the satisfaction of customers (internal or external)?

Tell me about how you did this in your last two jobs.

What do you think are the key needs and expectations of our customers?

In your most recent position, whom did you consider to be your primary customers? What were their needs or expectations?

Describe a time when you provided an exceptional level of customer service. What specifically did you do? What were the outcomes? Why was it exceptional?

What would your previous boss say about your commitment to satisfying the customer? In what ways did you fall short of providing excellent customer service?

In your view, how can the level of customer service provide a competitive advantage over my company's competitors (or, how did customer service provide a competitive advantage in your last two roles)?

Describe the benefits of good customer service. What are the advantages and what are the drawbacks to poor customer service?

The right answers reveal your commitment to customer service with specific examples to highlight times when you exceeded expectations.

Flexibility and Versatility

Talk about an experience you had where you needed to change your plan or approach to work on a project. What led to the change, and how did you react?

What would previous supervisors say about your capability to handle work requirements that are not routine or which change from day to day?

In your previous work, did you encounter multiple demands that needed to be met simultaneously? Talk about how you approached this work to meet these demands.

Describe a job or work situation that caused you to feel a lot of stress. Were you able to resolve the situation, and how did you do so?

The right answers reveal your experience with changing work demands, ability to multitask, ability to shift focus/effort as needed, and ability to react positively to change or stressful situations.

Integrity

Define what integrity means to you. How do you demonstrate integrity, both professionally and personally?

Give me some examples of how you have built trust or earned the respect of others. What kind of reputation do you have with your peers? What would they say if I asked them?

What will your previous one or two bosses say about your integrity? Further, what will they say about the extent to which you met commitments that you made to others and did what you said you would do?

Describe a time when you lost the trust of coworkers. What happened? What did you do? Why? What did you learn from that?

The right answers reveal a history of professional integrity, an understanding of the importance of trust in an organization, a history of personal integrity, and a commitment to follow through.

How Hard Are You Knocking?

Business Focus

In your current or previous position, describe how the company operated. How did it make money? What service did it provide to its customer base? How did your company's products or services provide business solutions for customers?

Describe your understanding of my company from a business perspective.

When evaluating proposed projects or products, what criteria do you use to determine if they are worthwhile or if they will generate a good return on investment?

In your past role, describe some of the key functions, divisions, or departments and what division you worked in. How did the various divisions affect each other?

In your previous one or two positions, how did you (or your position in general) specifically impact either the organization or department's bottom line? What actions had an impact on the organization's performance?

The right answers reveal your functional excellence, and your understanding of the drivers of business growth and profitability.

Creativity and Innovation

On a scale from 1 to 10, rate your level of creativity and innovative thinking. Why did you rate yourself there? Give specifics and justify your rating.

When was the last time you had a creative or innovative idea. What was it?

How would your past one or two bosses evaluate your creativity or ability to think outside the box when solving challenging problems?

Tell me about a time where you developed a new procedure or method that improved productivity. Provide specifics. What did you do? What was the outcome?

Talk about the importance of creativity and innovation in a company like mine.

If I were to observe you on the job for a couple of weeks and saw you at your creative best, what would I see you do?

The right answers reveal your ability to think outside the box, your appreciation for creativity and innovation, and a history of creative and innovative thinking in past roles.

Aptitude

What would your previous boss say about your ability to pick up things quickly and to learn new technologies, products, or services? Why would he or she say this? Give some examples from your past two positions.

What do you do to ensure continuous learning and to stay abreast of key developments in your field?

175

If someone were to ask you why you are an expert at your job, what would you tell him or her?

What do you do to stay informed about new products and services relevant to your job/career?

The right answers reveal your technical expertise, an ability to learn quickly, understanding of the key company products and services, and your ongoing interest in lifelong learning.

Multitasking and Prioritizing

Describe a time when you were working on two or more projects simultaneously. What did you do to ensure that you would accomplish both tasks accurately and on time? Give some specific examples.

What would your previous boss say about your ability to handle many responsibilities at one time and to prioritize effectively among them?

When you have many things going on at one time, how do you prioritize, and where do you focus your attention?

The right answers reveal your ability to balance multiple priorities at one time without compromising quality, a history of meeting multiple commitments simultaneously, and effective skill in prioritizing tasks to best maximize productivity.

Strategic Thinking

Have you ever participated in a strategic planning process? What did you learn from that experience?

What was the business strategy of your former employer? In your opinion, was it an effective one? Why or why not?

What are some key strategic issues that my company needs to consider as it moves forward? What about the particular group you are moving into: what are its strategic issues?

Have you ever been involved in a disciplined approach to strategic planning? Please describe it. What was the situation? What was your involvement? What was the outcome?

The right answers reveal your alignment of goals with corporate strategy and vision, ability to anticipate business challenges and opportunities, vision to see the big picture, and an understanding of the company's basic corporate strategy.

Three basic stages are associated with the interview:

- Preparation
- The interview
- Follow-up after the interview

PREPARATION/PRACTICE FOR THE INTERVIEW

The first step of preparing for an interview is to **review the exercises** you completed in the earlier chapters. Consider your personal and professional goals. Ask yourself some basic questions regarding your personal and professional life.

What are your goals in three years?

Where do you want to be in twenty years?

What are your strengths/weaknesses?

What is your greatest accomplishment? What did you learn from this?

What was your biggest defeat? What did you learn?

What did you like/dislike about your major?

What are your thoughts about relocation?

What is your desired salary?

What are your five greatest attributes?

What do you value in life?

Even if these questions are not asked in the interview, they help you further analyze your goals and therefore allow you to answer the interviewer's questions more easily and thoroughly.

Another action that might help your interview go smoothly is to **practice**. Talk in the mirror, to a friend, or in the shower. You need to prepare for interview questions such as, "What are your greatest strengths, weaknesses, or accomplishments? Why do you want to work here? Why should we hire you?" Be ready for the dreaded request to tell the employer about yourself. This is where your thirty-second commercial from the chapter on selling yourself will come in handy.

The next step is to **research the company**. Make sure you research the company thoroughly before you walk through its door. You will also have an advantage if you know information about the people who are interviewing you. Google them if you can or find them on LinkedIn.

Perhaps you will find a connection that can give you insider information. Know how long the company has been in existence, its growth in the past five years, how many people it employs, what it actually does, and most importantly, what you will do for the company.

Two of the biggest complaints that interviewers have are that candidates are unprepared to discuss the company, or know little about the company. Ask yourself how well you fit the company's culture and what your impact on this company would be. Why should they hire you? What can you bring to this company? Look at its strengths and match them to yours.

Everything you know about the company prior to interviewing contributes to your competitive edge. Do you think the other applicants for this position are doing extensive research on their potential employers? You need to make yourself stand out. If the interviewer asks, "Have you ever worked in small teams?" and you know that the company prides itself in small-team orientation projects, you can relate your experiences directly to the small group behavior.

You should also **prepare five to eight questions to ask the interviewer**. These questions could be about his or her position, the company's growth potential, or how the open position affects the long-term strategy of the company. Have these questions typed and in your small binder or padfolio. You may want to ask the interviewer if he or she would mind if you took notes during the interview. Sometimes you may want to write a few ideas, questions, or answers down during the interview to ask later.

Be well informed. Catch up on the latest news if you have not done so already. Pick up the morning paper or watch the evening news the night before. This topic may break the ice in the interview and illustrate that you are knowledgeable about current events. In addition, you may want to think of some items of discussion to break the ice yourself. For instance, you may notice the firm's new advertising campaign on television and comment on it. Avoid political or emotionally charged issues.

Give yourself the competitive advantage and learn as much about a company as you can. Everything you learn about a company can be used. Even if you don't receive a job offer, you may find that you have an interview with or even become employed by that firm's competitor at company B. You already know the weaknesses, strengths, and products of company A from your research. You are now in a position to intelligently discuss the industry and the particular competitors. Once the research is complete and you feel confident, the next step is the interview itself.

THE INTERVIEW

Be sure to **arrive on time** for your interview. Try to arrive about ten to fifteen minutes early if you can, because punctuality shows that you are responsible and dependable.

During the interview, remember to **be yourself**. Interviewers are looking for someone they like and who fits in well with the firm's culture, ideals and goals of the firm. Do not make things up or exaggerate. People know when you're lying, and you will lose not only your credibility with that interviewer, but more likely the job offer. These interviewers talk. They are all part of the interview team. Don't burn your bridges. Always be honest, and that integrity will remain with you.

Establish a **positive physical presence**. Greet the interviewer with a firm handshake and maintain comfortable eye contact, which gives a strong, confident first impression to the interviewer. During the interview, use good posture and sit up straight, which demonstrates confidence and pride. Also, be sure to always look the interviewer in the eye or just above the eye. Good eye contact reveals your eagerness to learn and your ability to listen.

The most important thing to remember about an interview is that you need to **be confident** and view this meeting as part of your overall networking game plan. In addition, you are the subject matter expert about yourself. Use this to your advantage and remain confident.

Interviewers are looking for the right person for their firm; you are looking for a job. They have pressure on them to perform for their firms, just as you are under pressure to perform for yourself. You have a lot in common with this new contact. This person is in a field that you enjoy. This person was in the same shoes as you at one time. They researched, interviewed, and were nervous. Go into the interview with the idea that no matter what happens, at least you will emerge knowing a little more about interviewing and with one more professional contact. The interviewer can be part of your network at a later date.

Remember that interviewing is a **two-way street**. The interviewer is trying to find out what they are getting. Who is this person? Why is this person here? Can this person do the job? Will this person stay with the firm? Will this person fit in with the corporate culture already in place?

In addition, you are testing yourself and learning if this job is what you are looking for. Will I be challenged? Will I learn? Do I fit into the company? Does the company fit me? These types of questions are the basic reasons you are interviewing. You may even find that you do not want to work for this company. Either way, you will walk away a better, more knowledgeable person, no matter what the outcome. An interview is just two people talking to and about each other. We all like to talk about ourselves, although many people are reticent to sell themselves in an interview. Get over it! You have earned the right to shine and to show what you are made of. Welcome the opportunity to challenge yourself and to stand above your competition to get the job.

You are most likely going to be asked questions about yourself. They will often be in-depth questions to illustrate how you handle various types of situations, and you are likely to be asked to cite occasions when you have demonstrated some specific ability. At this point, your experiences in organizations or internships can help you the most. Use what you have learned from your past experiences to sell yourself. Make sure you think about each question before you answer it. You do not want to be too aggressive and seem overbearing. There is no time limit, so take your time, listen, and answer the questions thoroughly.

You will get some tough questions during the interview such as describe your greatest strengths and weaknesses. Employers may look for all different answers here, but they are often curious as to how you view yourself and what you are doing to work on weaknesses. **Focus on the strengths** that are useful in the workplace and key to the firm's culture, such as being a team player, goal-oriented, or an effective problem solver. Be ready to defend these strengths with examples of situations when you demonstrated these abilities.

The weaknesses are a bit more difficult. You must **stay away from weaknesses** that will have anything to do with the prospective job, such as being stubborn, or fear of speaking or communicating your feelings.

Take the focus away from obvious weaknesses by saying, "As a new graduate, I do not have multiple years of experience. However, based on my leadership experience in my professional organizations and my ability to deal with teams, I feel that my people skills will expedite my ability to learn and adapt to your firm." Another good answer to a weakness question might be time management. "Since I was involved in multiple organizations, carried a full load and worked full time, I found that my weakness was time management, which is why I purchased this Blackberry to stay organized." Whatever your weakness, be sure to have some way of correcting it, and inform the interviewer that you are doing just that.

Be prepared for a question about **specific examples** of how you have handled various situations. To prepare for this, you may want to sit down a week before the interview and think about some situations in which you accomplished a goal or faced a conflict, failed, and learned from it, or made a tough choice. Be ready to share a leadership role you have had. Also, think about experiences that can answer a number of questions. For example, a project that revealed your creativity and teamwork may have also demonstrated your initiative. Of course, you don't want to repeat examples to questions but have a toolbox full of success stories that can highlight your talents from many perspectives.

Salary

Under no circumstances should you discuss possible salary figures in your first interview.

An interviewer may ask what type of salary you are looking for. A good response is a brief statement such as, "I am considering many opportunities with a few firms and am more interested in understanding the role and responsibilities of the position than the starting salary of the position. What is the salary range that accompanies this position?" Salary negotiations are not dealt with until you have an actual job offer, which usually does not come until after several interviews. Once the job has been offered, try to ask for a few days to decide. Do not jump at it. In those few days, you can evaluate the job offer, responsibilities, corporate culture, and opportunities for growth.

Your Questions for the Interviewer

After you have answered the interviewer's questions, you then have the opportunity to ask some of your own. Try to use questions that relate to the research you uncovered. Use the questions you wrote prior to the interview or ask questions that you have thought of since the interview started. Although you have written your questions on paper, you should still have them committed to memory.

Here are some examples of good interview questions:

Through my research, I have found that XYZ Corporation has grown twenty-three percent in the last year. What steps is the firm taking to ensure this continued growth (new products, mergers, strategic alliances)?

What type of training programs and professional development do you offer to new employees?

What is the evaluation/performance review or measurement process for this position?

What type of person will be successful in this position?

What are some of the goals of the firm for the next five years?

What are three tasks I would need to accomplish to be successful in my first six months?

Apply the answers to these questions to your employment decisions. Remember, you are interviewing the company as much as they are interviewing you. Later, you can list all the pros and cons that were revealed during your interviews and evaluate the material to make a fully educated decision about the company where you would like to work.

The Second Interview

Once the first face-to-face interview is complete, the interviewer will probably want you to return for a second interview, which is very common. During the second interview, you might meet with a new set of people, including the team with which you would be working. You may also meet with the individuals who interact with this position. Focus on the same guidelines as the first interview. Relax and remember that your job is to continue to gather good information to help you determine whether the position is a good fit for you.

The second interview is also the time to discuss position and company specifics with the interviewer. We recommend asking detailed questions about the position as well as the company benefits. Always secure a copy of the position description before interviewing.

Here are some questions to help you better understand the job position:

What type of training will be offered?

Can you explain the reporting structure and leadership structure for this position?

What are your expectations for the position?

What are the critical success factors for this position?

What would I need to accomplish in my first six months to be successful?

186

Questions to ask in order to get a better understanding of the company's benefits:

What type of health care benefits does the firm offer?

What is the monthly insurance premium for single and/or married employees?

What type of life insurance does your firm offer?

Does the firm offer tuition reimbursement?

Does your firm offer a 401(k) retirement plan? If so, with what company?

Does your firm match my 401(k) contribution?

Does your company offer stock options?

What is the vacation policy?

Does this position have a bonus opportunity?

Does your firm have an orientation program?

Does your firm have a career development process?

FOLLOW-UP AFTER THE INTERVIEWS

After you have completed the interviews, follow up with a thank-you note. Do not procrastinate—do this on the same day. Do it as soon as you get home.

How Hard Are You Knocking?

We recommend mailing a thank-you note to everyone who interviewed you. We prefer a handwritten thank-you note because it differentiates you and is more thoughtful than a typed letter or an email.

However, if you do not feel comfortable with a handwritten letter or if you have poor handwriting, send a well-written typed letter that references a few topics discussed during the interview as well as your interest in the position.

Your thank-you note is also your opportunity to answer any questions left hanging after the interview, clarify any answers, or elaborate on one of your strengths you neglected to mention. If you feel like time is limited, send a quick email thank-you note and then follow up with a hard copy.

Sample typewritten thank-you note

EMILY B. A. MANAGER

430 MAIN STREET

PLEASANTON, CALIFORNIA 65588

555-255-4227 MBA@YOURISP.EDU

September 1, 2010

Mr. Jack Donaghy

Regional Director of Human Resources

Capital Corporation

Naperville, Illinois 33333

Dear Mr. Donaghy:

Thank you for spending time with me today to discuss the position of marketing manager of the residential accounts division.

It was a great pleasure to meet you and to learn more about how I could contribute to the long-term success and growth of Capital Corporation. In particular, the Canadian expansion strategy is very exciting, and with my experience of having lived in Montreal for five years, I'm sure that I could be an effective team member and meet or exceed all quarterly goals.

I look forward to hearing from you at your earliest convenience.

Sincerely,

Emily B. A. Manager

CHAPTER 10

CLOSING THE DEAL

NEXT STEPS AND EXPECTATIONS

You've had your interviews and followed up with a thank-you note. Your next step will probably be to wait.

During this stage of the game, the key word is **patience**. Don't communicate too much and risk presenting yourself as desperate. Often, the interviewer tells you during the interview the time frame for making a decision or what the hiring process entails. You may receive a call in a week or have literature sent to you in the mail. The interviewer may set up the next interview right then (if applicable). Your job is to find out as many details as you can about the process. If interviewers tell you that they will call you in a week or so, try to ask them to specify a certain day.

You may ask if you could contact them if they have not called you. If you do not have any response in the amount of time specified (or about two weeks if no time is specified), contact them. At that point, ask the interviewer about the status of the position and say that you want to confirm your interest and your fit for the job. In addition, ask them about their expectations regarding the decision, because you are interviewing with other organizations, which seem to be moving faster than expected.

This moment is a tricky one. You do not want to push the hiring manager or sound desperate. However, at the same time you want to show that you are in demand. An expected wait of one to two weeks could stretch to three to four weeks. Be patient and don't panic!

REJECTION

Rejection is a part of life and something we all face at one time or another. If you are not selected for a position, you will most likely receive a letter to this effect. Such letters often say that the company hired a "more qualified" candidate. However, the most qualified person is not necessarily who gets the job; it is the person who knows how to market himself or herself, the person who knows what needs to be done to be successful during the interview. Make sure this person is you! Learn from your mistakes and use this experience to gain this knowledge. Henry Ford once said, "Failure is the opportunity to begin again more intelligently." Do not let rejection discourage you. Walt Disney was fired from a newspaper because he lacked ideas. You need to continue to drive forward.

What should you do if you are turned down?

First, don't be discouraged. You may not have enjoyed working for that company anyway. Perhaps the company saw that your personality did not fit its culture and that you would have ended up leaving.

Second, send a follow-up letter thanking the interviewer and the company for the opportunity to meet and interview with them. This step keeps your name on their minds.

Third, be sure to continue to follow up with other companies to whom you have sent your resume or have pending interviews. Keep your opportunities open.

Finally, do not be afraid to interview with this company later. Often, you may not have met some qualifications such as practical experience. The next time you interview with this company, your competition for the position may be different, and the people making the decision to hire may be different as well.

Although this might be difficult, try to contact the interviewer who interviewed you and ask for advice on what you could do to improve. Don't be surprised if employers decline to give feedback. Remember, take constructive criticism and use it to your benefit. The interviewer may give you some beneficial points before you interview again. You can contact the person by phone or by sending them a letter. Either way, follow up with some of the interviewers whom you think may give you constructive feedback. However, do not do this for every interview because you may get overwhelmed, which could lead to frustration and cause you to end the search process.

Sample questions for your follow-up letter after a rejection might include:

Could you please provide me with some areas in which you think I need improvement?

Could you please provide me with constructive criticism to help me with the interview process?

Could you give some pointers on interviewing and on things on which I could improve?

We all need to learn from our mistakes, and the interviewing arena is perfect for learning about the business world from the ground floor. Don't be surprised if hiring managers will not give you frank feedback. They may feel like they have more to lose than gain by helping you.

NEGOTIATION AND ACCEPTANCE

Negotiating for a starting salary is very difficult and often the most stressful aspect of finding a new job. The balance between the stress of needing the job and the art of negotiating the starting salary is often the balancing act. When you are negotiating a starting salary for a new job, knowing the appropriate starting salary and successful negotiating techniques is invaluable.

Keep in mind that the recruiter, interviewer, or hiring manager has the advantage. In most cases, the recruiter brings years of salary and benefits negotiation experience. They have a pay range in mind that is unknown to you but do possess the ability to manipulate that pay range if absolutely necessary. This is the reason that you need to do as much research as possible.

Education is your best defense. The art of salary negotiation is preparation.

Research everything you can to find information on market wages and a competitive salary for your job, industry, and geographic region—online resources, employment surveys, libraries, professional organizations, and peers.

In addition to compensation figures, there are a number of other items that can be negotiated. Make sure you understand the total benefit package as well. Research the average number of vacation days and / paid time off. Understand the cost of healthcare benefit premiums, vision insurance, and dental coverage. You should understand the company's 401(k) retirement match and have a good understanding of the firm's training and tuition reimbursement policy for such items as certifications, training classes and advanced degrees.

Below are a set of tips and guidelines that will help with your preparation.

- **Don't discuss salary until you are offered the job**

You do not want to anchor the interviewer to a specific number, especially if you announce a lower number than they were willing to offer. It is not in your best interest to talk about your starting salary. When an employer asks, "What are your salary requirements?" or "What are you currently earning?" they are gathering information on your compensation expectations. If you provide a number that is too high you might be screened out. If you present a number that is too low you'll

195

lose money in the initial offer, or you'll be eliminated as under-qualified based on your low salary requirements.

When asked about your salary expectation during the interview phase, we recommend simply responding with, "Salary is not my motivator at this point. I would like to understand the role and responsibilities of the position and expect that the compensation range would reflect a fair market wage."

When salary is discussed, let the employer talk first. If the employer does push to understand your salary requirement, provide a bracketed salary range such as $45,000 – $55,000. You should always preface each salary comment with, "Based on my research"—such as, "Based on my research, a marketing analyst position in Chicago ranges from $45,000 to $55,000."

In many entry-level jobs, salary is not negotiable. If salary is not negotiable, try to work in perks or better benefits. In today's environment and economy, items that do not directly impact a company's immediate cash flow are sometimes the easiest to include in an offer such as additional vacation days, flextime, or the ability to telecommute from home.

• **Resources to use**

Below are some online resources that that we have found to be very helpful when researching potential salary ranges:

- www.Payscale.com
- www.jobstar.org

- www.monster.salary.com
- www.salary.com
- www.indeed.com
- www.salaryexpert.com
- www.careerbuilder.com
- www.glassdoor.com
- www.collegegrad.com
- www.rileyguide.com
- www.mycareer.com
- www.nace.org
- www.Salarywizard.com
- www.Benefitslink.com

Keep in mind that the employer will likely view compensation data differently than the employee. Two common points the employer may wish to discuss are:

1. The sources used to obtain the data in the report.

2. Whether the data in the report matches your job profile, years of experience required, the company profile (private or public), and job location.

When you use any resource, just make sure you are comparing apples to apples. Use your best judgment when reviewing salary figures on the web. Make sure the figures are from a credible source. Far too often, salary figures are misrepresented on the Internet to draw attention to an open position. In addition, you should find one of the many surveys conducted relating to this subject, which are categorized by industry and job title.

Consider the other benefits that the company also provides such as health care benefits, vacation, and flextime, and/or tuition reimbursement. Most companies provide a range of other benefits, sometimes valued as more important that simply an annual salary. When you evaluate a job offer, there is much to consider. Only you can evaluate the importance of base salary, vacation time, a shorter commute, or great healthcare benefits. Review the general list of categories below when evaluating additional benefits:

- Vacation time

    Do you have to wait a year to receive 1 week of vacation?

    Is vacation time dictated by the number of years you have been with the firm?

    - 1-2 years: 2 weeks of vacation
    - 3-10 years: 3 weeks of vacation
    - 10+ years: 4 weeks of vacation

- Paid time off

    What is the policy for paid time off?

    How are sick days counted and are they combined with vacation time?

- Holidays

    How many holidays does the company recognize and pay you for?

- Retirement

  Is there a 401(k) retirement plan?

  Is there a company 401(k) match for each dollar you contribute?

  What is the limit to contribute to the firm's 401(k) plan?

  Is there a pension plan?

- Life and disability insurance

  Is there a cost to life and disability insurance? *i.e.* pays full cost of life insurance coverage equal to a full year's salary.

  Is there an option to add additional life insurance?

  Does the company provide disability insurance that typically pays a percent of salary if employee is unable to work?

- Medical insurance

  What is the cost to medical coverage?

  Does the employer pay all or part of premiums on policy that covers health claims?

  What are the costs for routine physical and prescriptions?

  Is there a deductable?

- Tuition assistance

  Does the firm provide tuition reimbursement for certifications or advanced degrees?

  Does the company pay for all or most of job-related classes or certifications?

- Stock purchase or savings plan

  Are there stock options?

Are the options priced below market value and are there contribution matches available?

• Child care

Does the company provide preschool or daycare services?

Does the company have a Flexible Spending Account (FSA), which allows you to withhold dollars tax-free to pay for childcare or medical coverage?

Negotiating a salary may be impossible—the hiring manager may say, "Take it or leave it." However, it is usually in your best interest to try to negotiate. Recognize that the employer will probably try to offer you as little money as possible, or may have a budget-defined salary for an entry-level position. You probably need to make a judgment call. In most cases, the employer has a starting point and a maximum offer. This range fluctuates with position but can be negotiated. Do your homework, see what the average salary is for that position, and even convey to the employer if the offer is below the average salary for that position. Once the recruiter offers you the position, start the negotiation process. Consider the following negotiating tips.

Negotiation Tips

• Never accept on the spot. When the interviewer offers you the job, tell the interviewer that you are very interested but you need to discuss it with your family. This will give you time to think about the offer.

- Tell the interviewer that you will call him or her in a few days to provide an answer. This time is the best for negotiating. They are eager for you to accept.

- Negotiating over the phone can sometimes be your best strategy. Start with at least ten percent above the offer. Typically, most interviewers have the authority to negotiate. When you call, explain to the interviewer that you are interested in the position, but, based on your research, you were expecting $ X (which should equal ten percent above the offer). In some cases, the offer might be solid with no room to move. In that case, accept the position if it matches that company criteria you established at the beginning of this book and ask for a performance and wage review after six months of employment.

- Keep in mind that you are negotiating the entire compensation package, not just base salary. Total compensation involves base salary, bonuses, and benefits. Keep this in perspective as you evaluate the offer.

ACCEPTING AN OFFER

There are a number of factors in evaluating job offers.

The role and job responsibility

Fully understand the nature of the work and make sure you review the role and responsibly of the position. Request a copy of the position description, which is a document that provides details associated with typical tasks and activities, the type of internal and external clients you might face and the type of work you will be expected to perform. Here are a few questions you should ask when evaluating the nature of the work:

Do I like the industry?

Do I admire the products or services of the employer?

Is this job interesting to me?

Does this position match my career plans and personal goals?

Your boss and team

You will be spending a significant portion of your day with your boss and your team. It is important that you consider the culture of the firm, the chemistry of the group and the interpersonal and management style of your boss or manager.

The other factors that should be considered during this evaluation might include the work / life balance or the typical workweek balanced against personal or family commitments. Consider the geographic location of the position and the time spent commuting and access to family and friends.

Below is a general list that we use when working with college graduates and individuals interested in a career change.

The Industry

- Is the firm in an industry that is growing in this economy?
- What type of growth potential exists in their industry?
- What are the future needs for goods and services the firm currently provide?
- Is the industry seasonal or does the industry depend on a specific business cycle?
- Does the company work for the government or depend on government policies and programs?
- What are the long-term opportunities exist within the industry that the firm operates?

The Company

- What is the reputation of my employer?
- Is my firm viewed as innovative and technically savvy?
- What is the management style of my firm?
- What is the financial stability of the firm? (Have they had layoffs or had to restructure)
- What is the reputation of the executive management?
- Is the employer publicly traded or a private firm?
- Is the company well established or a new start-up venture?
- Who are the clients / prospects of the organization?

The Position

- What are the duties and responsibilities and do they match my interests and skills?

- What is the culture like? What are the personalities of managers and team members?
- What is the scope of my work and what type of variety do my assignments provide?
- What is the opportunity for individual achievement? How are performance reviews conducted?
- What are my opportunities for growth and advancement?
- What type of training and continuing education opportunities exist in the role?
- What are the expectations of me in this new role and how are these measured?
- What type of interaction will I have with mentors and influential team members?
- What are the working conditions and will I work independently or part of a team?
- Do I have an opportunity to travel? If so, what is the frequency?
- What type of incentives are part of this role? (Overtime, bonuses, etc)
- How do the other employees like working in the company? What type of turnover does the firm have?
- What type of intellectual stimulation will I have in my job and on my team?

The location

- Where is the position located?
- What is the cost of living in the geographic area?
- What is the commute time to the firm's location from where I live?
- What is the community like in the location?
- Where is the company headquartered and does the company have regional offices?
- Does the company operate domestically and / or internationally?
- Is there an opportunity to relocate to another office?
- Is there an opportunity to relocate to a different country?

Once you decide on the offer and want to accept it, verbally accept and write an acceptance letter to the individual offering you the position. In addition, send a letter to all of the interviewers that you met with during the interview process, stating that you have accepted and are excited about working with the organization. This step is what the job search is all about: accepting a job offer. Remember that your reputation follows you everywhere you go, so you should never burn your bridges. Pay close attention to detail and follow up with diligence. Always give 100 percent, and ultimately you will succeed.

Chapter Checklist

✓ I can effectively answer the "tell me about yourself" question.

✓ I am prepared to answer questions that describe my qualifications.

✓ I have written out answers to common interview questions and have memorized compelling responses.

✓ I know how to research my interviewer.

✓ I will prepare at least five to ten questions that reveal my research and curiosity about the company.

✓ I know what the average salary ranges are for the jobs I'm seeking.

An example of an acceptance letter is on the following page.

Acceptance Letter Example

JANE DOE ADEAR

555 East Third Street

Jacksonville, Florida 22222

(555) 567-0000 doeadear@isp.com

April 10, 2010

Mr. Greg Jones

Business Manager

SalesMonger Inc.

1234 White St.

Cleveland, Ohio 99998

Dear Greg:

This letter is to accept the position of sales associate with SalesMonger, Inc. I am most excited about this opportunity, and I'm sure the position will be challenging and rewarding. I believe strongly in the corporate philosophy of SalesMonger and in the quality and integrity of the brand and its products.

Thank you for giving me this opportunity. I am confident that I can make a significant contribution to the growth and success of the firm.

Best regards,

Jane Doe Adear

CHAPTER 11

DID YOU CHOOSE THE RIGHT JOB?

Congratulations! Your job search is complete, and you have succeeded in finding a new job. As you settle into your new office, cube, or desk and receive your office supplies, use this book for one last piece of advice.

For new graduates we must warn you that the work world is considerably different from the collegiate world. While you won't be graded as frequently, your yearly evaluations will be very important. You may wish you had more input on your work and be surprised when a good job is met with silence.

Have realistic expectations. If this is your first position out of college, understand that you will need to work your way up. Everyone starts somewhere, and if you are in a less-than-inspiring administrative job, commit to doing your best. Be on time, do your work and ask for more assignments. Have a strategy. Figure out what skills you can acquire in your present job that will help you with future positions. Take any course that is offered from Customer Service 101 to Advanced Excel. Learn as much as you can. You will impress your supervisors and prepare yourself for your next position.

This chapter will help you successfully transition into your new job. There are crucial skills to master and knowledge to gain early on. Avoid deadly mistakes. Don't miss the opportunity to build a foundation of success from your first day.

And, perhaps most importantly, to find out if this is the right job for you.

THE FIRST 90 DAYS

Based on our experience and research, we have found the assimilation or orientation period for any new employee is the most critical time to make a positive first impression. The following detailed outline should assist you in making the transition as smooth as possible. This outline focuses on five parts of the organization you need to understand within your first ninety days of employment:

1. Company knowledge
2. Position knowledge
3. Product/service knowledge
4. Process/political knowledge
5. Personal growth and effectiveness.

Use this outline as a frame of reference when planning your days and scheduling time with your supporting leader or peers.

Your first step is to make sure that you understand the position description and your superior's expectations. Set up a regular time to check in and see how you are performing.

MASTER THE COMPANY

The first area of the business that you need to understand is the company itself. Do your best to fully understand the organization's **history**.

How did the firm get started and who were its first customers? Try to learn the organization's **mission statement** and understand how it applies to the company, your team, and your specific position.

Company values are also very important to understand. These guiding principles help illustrate how the culture is managed, how decisions are made, how customers are serviced, and how the leadership group should perform.

In addition, as part of any orientation program, understand the **structure** of the organization, which tells you who reports to whom and how groups within the company work together. An organizational structure is also a good starting point for you to develop your career development plan by identifying possible positions that interest you. Within the organizational structure, you need to understand the roles and responsibilities of your peers, managers, internal customers, and suppliers.

Finally, you need to understand **office logistics**. If you need a new stapler, where do you go, and how do you order it? What are the software programs that you need to understand and use on a daily basis? These tools can include a scheduling and email system, desktop publishing programs, and/or an internal customer relationship management system.

Use this list to help organize your learning and orientation of company knowledge:

- ✓ Company or organizational history
- ✓ Mission, values, and vision
- ✓ Company culture
- ✓ Organizational structure
- ✓ People: roles and responsibilities
- ✓ Office logistics/technology

MASTER YOUR POSITION

The next phase of your orientation program is gaining position knowledge. You need to understand and confirm the role and responsibilities of your position and understand the types of tasks for which you will be responsible. In addition, you should ask the human resources department for a copy of a **position description**. If you manage other employees, ask for their position descriptions as well. These documents outline roles and responsibilities and provide a framework of overall accountability.

Find out what **current projects** you are responsible for and the timing and expectations of these projects.

We also recommend contacting a peer within the company for a **position meeting**. During this meeting, try to understand his or her role, responsibilities, and position expectations. In some cases, we recommend conducting meetings with everyone with whom you would interact, including your internal suppliers or employees who supply you with information, content, and/or materials.

You should also try to meet your **internal customers**. Who are your customers? What are their expectations of you and your role?

Finally, you need to fully understand the **critical success factors** of your position. What will you be measured against to ensure your success? You should work with your managers to understand their expectations as well as the performance review process of your firm. To be successful, you need to understand how you are evaluated and reviewed for future promotions and salary raises.

Review this list of topics for your position orientation:

- ✓ Confirm role and responsibilities
- ✓ Projects and tasks
- ✓ Position expectations
- ✓ Success measurements
- ✓ Performance review process

MASTER THE COMPANY PRODUCT AND/OR SERVICES

Once you feel that you have a solid grip on the company and a full understanding of your position and organization's expectation, you need to develop a plan to learn about the products and services your company produces and sells. Do your best to fully understand all of the products and services within your firm and the history behind the products. In some cases, a cursory review of the products and services is sufficient. However, if you are dealing with these products on a daily basis, you need to fully understand the product specifications. The quicker you are up to speed, the more successful you will be.

Make sure you document your learning through this phase. You will need to reference the information multiple times. If this learning takes place through a formal class or you have to schedule one-on-one time with a product expert, view this knowledge as an invaluable asset to your career growth within the firm. Read as much information within the internal and external websites as well as any marketing material you can gather.

By understanding product features and attributes, you will be a more successful team player and well positioned within the firm for programs such as a fast-track program. As part of this phase, you should also gain a better understanding of your market segments and the industries your firm targets.

You also need to understand the firm's current customers as well as prospects. Develop a **customer list and/or customer profile** as you learn more. As you read about customers through case studies or press releases, save the information into a profile to reference later. Again, this information is an important asset to career growth.

Here is the list for your product/services orientation:

- ✓ Product/service history
- ✓ Products, features, and attributes
- ✓ Product training program
- ✓ Industries, customers, and prospects

MASTER THE COMPANY POLITICS

In preparing for a new career and settling into the firm, new employees often overlook one area: **political/process knowledge.** Any new employee experiences a period of initiation. In order to make a positive first impression, however, you need to understand the who holds influential power in the team or company so that you do not step into any land mines or on anyone's toes.

The best way to approach this phase is to **identify possible allies.** Perhaps it's the boss who hired you (although that does not tend to sit well with existing employees). Alternatively, this ally could be a peer within your department or even outside the group. The criteria you should use to identify potential allies are based on tenure, reputation, and influence. Often times, the employee who has been there a long time and is well liked by many is the best ally or mentor.

Through our experiences, we have found that this step is often the most important. For example, we hired a senior executive in our firm who started his first day by challenging a peer in public. As with any organization, the news quickly spread, and this person's reputation was tarnished from day one. He was probably very good at his job, but no one gave him a chance in fear that he would turn on them as well. He lasted six months.

However, there is some good news. All new employees usually have a honeymoon period during which the company typically overlooks missteps or political mistakes. New employees are simply corrected or given advice to help them navigate through the political arena. Just think about when you started at a new school. The school had groups or cliques that spent their time building relationships as well as their reputation. Work is no different. Every company has processes, procedures, and norms. Some of these processes are well documented while others are silent norms and cultures.

Do your best to understand your boundaries and the boundaries of your position and team. Spend your first ninety days learning, listening, and building relationships. This time and activity will serve you well in establishing a successful work environment.

MASTER YOUR OWN PROFESSIONAL EFFECTIVENESS

The final area where you need to focus your energies is on your own professional effectiveness. Use your **performance review results** to help improve your personal and professional performance.

Perhaps target **educational opportunities** such as formal education, training, seminars, or certifications. As you grow within your position and firm, continually improve your personal effectiveness skills. Use the orientation process to help you formulate your strategy and specific steps that need to be done to build an individual career development plan.

A section earlier in this book outlined specific criteria you should consider when identifying your target companies. A formal **career development program** should be high on your list of desired factors for potential employers. In order for you to continually grow within your firm, you need to have a **plan of action** that should include expanding the breadth of your current role and identifying other potential positions within the firm you should target.

Your career is your responsibility. Make sure you are continually improving your personal effectiveness skills. In some companies, you need to work with human resources, while in others the management team is well trained and expected to coach their employees.

Consider which topics on this list need to be on your priority list:

Business writing

Presentation skills

Listening skills

Project management

Interpersonal communication

Problem-solving skills

Time management

Creativity

Integrity and ethics

Flexibility/adaptability

Achievement orientation

Business acumen

Facilitation skills

Interviewing skills

Conflict resolution

Building a high-performance team /supervisory skills

Decision making

Process development

Coaching and mentoring

Financial management

Delegation and empowerment

Industry knowledge

Organization skills

Technical knowledge

Insider's Tip: Your career is your responsibility. Make sure you are continually improving your personal effectiveness skills.

As your progress in your career endeavors, make sure you continually improve your personal effectiveness. In our work as professional career coaches, we are often asked the question, "When will I know that it is time to move to another job, position, or company?" The advice we give to all of our clients is to focus on three aspects of your development:

1. Personal satisfaction

2. Professional development

3. Financial reward

We understand that the grass sometimes seems greener in other companies or in other positions. However, if you are focusing on these three developmental needs, you are managing your career effectively.

PERSONAL SATISFACTION

The first developmental area is your personal satisfaction. Do you enjoy your work? Do you like the people you work with? Does the company culture, team, or peer group that you work with personally stimulate you? Are your personal educational goals being met at your current company? You need to consider these types of questions when evaluating your personal developmental needs. You spend the majority of your life at work. Therefore, you need to personally enjoy the environment and be continually motivated to strive for excellence.

PROFESSIONAL DEVELOPMENT

The second developmental area is your professional development. You should always be professionally challenged in your job. These challenges can come in many forms, such as a high quota, difficult learning curve, or the task of managing multiple people.

Ask yourself if you are receiving opportunities to learn and grow within your position or role within the firm. Do you feel professionally stimulated with your projects, tasks, or contributions to the firm? Have you developed and communicated to your supporting leader a professional career development plan? We often ask these types of questions to professionals who consider leaving a position because they do not feel professionally challenged.

FINANCIAL REWARD

The final developmental area you need to evaluate is your financial reward. Financial needs include base salary, bonus opportunities, and benefits provided by a firm. Through our experience, we realize that most people do not feel they are ever paid enough for the value they bring to a firm. However, do you feel you are paid a market-based salary for your position, education, experience level, and responsibility? Do you feel your bonus opportunity is realistic at your firm? Do you feel that the benefits offered at your firm match the market standards? Do you feel that your vacation time is adequate compared to the market?

You need to evaluate these types of questions to review your financial developmental needs. Often times, people change jobs or accept jobs strictly for financial reasons. Research conducted through organizational surveys, focus groups, and interviews shows that, for employees overall, financial rewards appear seventh among valued attributes of an organization.

Based on our findings, the top ten most valued attributes of an organization include:

1. Stability

2. Organizational culture and environment

3. Employee morale

4. Leadership practices

5. Leader/employee relations

6. Performance feedback

7. Compensation and benefits

8. Growth and opportunity

9. Company innovation

10. Product quality

While an important aspect of a job, compensation is not considered the primary motivator for people who leave or accept new employment. As you are researching organizations, evaluating companies, or entertaining a job offer, make sure you are considering all aspects of the position and company.

This holistic approach benefits you in the long run. If you are professionally challenged and personally motivated, the financial rewards will follow.

Chapter Checklist

✓ I have a game plan for my first 90 days.

✓ I will contact my network and share my good job news with them.

✓ I will develop key allies within my first 90 days.

✓ I will keep in regular touch with my broader network

✓ I will keep track of my accomplishments.

✓ I will attend to areas where I can improve.

CHAPTER 12

MANAGING YOUR CAREER

In today's economy, you will need to keep on knocking throughout your career. Be proactive in managing your career so you will know how to find open doors again and again.

As you continue to grow and prosper in your new job, maintain your focus on your career growth. The days of being employed by one company for your entire career are over. In today's fast-moving economy, the average job tenure is between three to five years; in other words, in three to five years, you will likely be looking for another opportunity. Therefore, you need to continue to build your network and sharpen your skills for your next career move. Keep this book as a resource for your next search, and implement the following guidelines as you manage your career.

STAY CONNECTED WITH YOUR NETWORK

As mentioned in the networking chapter, you need to continually stay in contact with your network. Schedule time to make phone calls just to keep in touch. Schedule lunches with those key contacts to stay abreast of their career activities as well. As with any new job, you want to focus your energies on your tasks at hand, but do not forget to stay involved in your networking roundtables, industry and alumni associations, and social groups.

Your network of family, friends, and business associates should continue to grow as you expand your career. Remember, networking refers to a social activity typically utilizing reciprocal relationships to facilitate communication between people.

Networking can be a very powerful tool to build skills and capabilities and develop access to opportunities and information. Build and save your database of contacts and continue to grow and expand the breadth of your network. Leverage your experiences and network of contacts to help others meet new people, gather information, or find a new job.

Insider's Tips: I often talk on the phone during my commute time to stay connected to my network. This is the perfect "downtime" to stay in touch.

STAY CONNECTED TO YOUR INDUSTRY AND PROFESSION

Make sure you stay abreast of your changing industry. Stay involved in industry associations and professional organizations. Continue to build your knowledge of the industry through educational workshops, seminars, or trade journals. You have no guarantee that your company will stay independent or financially viable. You might be forced to look for a new job if your company merges, files for Chapter 11, or downsizes. You need to continue to build your knowledge and skills in your industry, thus continuing to increase your marketability. Don't forget your contacts in professional recruiting and staffing firms. Send them good referrals to keep in contact.

CONTINUE TO BUILD YOUR PERSONAL EFFECTIVENESS SKILLS

You are the only person who can manage your career. You need to make sure you are furthering your personal effectiveness skills. These skills refer to your formal education such as acquiring an MBA or professional certifications as well as enhancing your position competencies, business acumen, presentation skills, and leadership effectiveness skills.

UPDATE YOUR MASTER RESUME AT LEAST ONCE A YEAR

As your career advances do not forget to capture your expanded job responsibilities, key accomplishments, successful projects, and significant results.

A TALE OF TWO JOB SEEKERS: SUSAN VS. MIKE

To further illustrate the suggestions about keeping yourself connected and marketable, let us share with you the stories of two people who managed their careers quite differently.

225

After college, Susan joined a company that was growing and appeared to have a wonderful future. She worked hard, climbed the company ladder, and increased her earnings threefold. She was in the office early and stayed late. She earned a reputation in the company as a real winner and great contributor.

As the years progressed, Susan continued to focus all her energy on her job. She didn't meet new people outside of those who worked for the company. She dropped her membership in the industry associations and even discontinued her connections to her alumni association. Her network of people began to shrink, and her knowledge of everything except the narrow world of her company slowly slipped into the realm of historical data. In fact, we heard people refer to her as a "dinosaur."

Everything about Susan was what she accomplished in the past, and nothing about her was current. In the same way that never using your muscles causes them to shrink and deteriorate, Susan's market value and personal network were withering.

After fifteen years with the company that Susan helped grow, the company was purchased by a competitor, which was great news for the owners but bad news for Susan. Her services were no longer needed, and she was out looking for a job. Her network was nonexistent, and her skills were outdated.

In many ways, Susan was in no better shape for a job search than she was fifteen years before when she was a fresh graduate. It took her a year and a half to find a new job. She took a position that was lower in both salary and responsibility. If Susan continues to follow her narrow path of focus, she will most likely repeat her marginally successful career track.

In contrast, consider Mike's story. Mike, like Susan, was a young college graduate. He accepted a position with a large firm that had opportunities galore. Mike followed a much different path than Susan. He worked hard in the office but continued to keep a healthy focus on both growing his personal network and continuing to improve his personal effectiveness. Using the tuition reimbursement program offered by his firm, he enrolled in the local Executive MBA program, and on his own time in a weekend program over the course of three years he earned his MBA.

Mike also remained active in the college alumni association in the city where he lived, accepting the position of president of the local chapter. It took additional time to handle this position, but the contacts he made were immensely valuable. Mike was skilled at not only meeting and greeting people, but also taking the time to enter their names in his personal database. He was creative about keeping in touch with everyone he met. Whether it was a holiday card or a phone call to ask a question of someone who might be more qualified, Mike stayed connected.

Mike seemed to squeeze so much into his week: lunch with someone from the Alumni Club, an evening meeting at his church to help with the new expansion plans, and golf with a group of business peers on Saturday. Mike was so well connected that we even called him at times to see if he could help us network to specific companies that we wanted to know better.

After six years in his first position, the company merged with a larger firm, and new management changed the culture.

Mike was ready to move on. With the grace and speed of a deer, Mike put the word out through his network that he was interested in seeking a new opportunity. We can only imagine how people would describe Mike as they spread the word. "I know a guy who would be fantastic for any company that would be lucky enough to get him. He is smart, just earned his MBA, and is a very well-rounded professional." Within a few weeks, Mike had the opportunity to meet with several companies that wanted to recruit him.

Exactly thirty-seven days after Mike decided to move on, he was sitting in his new office! Of course the first thing Mike did that night was email his entire network letting them know of his new position, his new contact information, and how much he appreciated their help.

Follow Mike's example. Be proactive about your career management. Don't put your career in jeopardy by neglecting to attend to your professional growth and networking. Keep this book on your bookshelf, ready to use again in three to five years. Keep your career healthy by building your personal network and continuing to learn.

Keep on knocking!

"Somehow I can't believe that there are any heights that can't be scaled by a man who knows the secrets of making dreams come true.

This special secret, it seems to me, can be summarized in four Cs. They are curiosity, confidence, courage, and constancy, and the greatest of all is confidence. When you believe in a thing, believe in it all the way, implicitly, and unquestionably." —*Walt Disney*